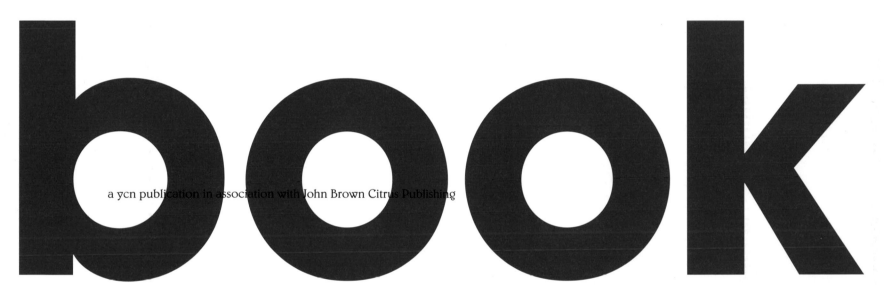

book

a ycn publication in association with John Brown Citrus Publishing

John
Brown
Citrus
Publishing

John Brown Citrus Publishing
The New Boathouse
136-142 Bramley Road
London W10 6SR
Tel: 020 7565 3000
email: info@jbcp.co.uk
www.jbcp.co.uk
Editor Andrew Losowsky
Deputy Creative Director
Chris Parker
Designers Corinna Drossel,
Damian Good
Sub-editor Jeremy White
Production Sue Harper
Publisher Andy Roughton
Senior Picture editor
Graham Harper
Picture editor Sally Ryall
Picture researcher Laura Jones
IT Manager Richard Sacre
Thoughts photographer
Annie Collinge
Colour origination
John Brown Citrus Publishing
Printer Rotolito Lombarda
Paper M-real
Published by YCN and John Brown
Citrus Publishing © 2004
Creative Director Jeremy Leslie
Managing Director
Dean Fitzpatrick
Chief Executive Andrew Hirsch
Chairman John Brown
No part of this book may be
reproduced without permission.
The views expressed within are not
necessarily those of ycn
or the publishers.

ISBN 0-9548597-0-7

04.05

ycn

Young Creatives Network
1st Floor
181 Cannon Street Road
London
E1 2LX
Tel: 020 7702 0700
email: info@ycnonline.com
www.ycnonline.com
Creative and Editorial Director
Nick Defty
Commercial Director Dr Ben Saw
Web Development Daniel Howells
Education Executives
Edward Baker and Caroline Swanne
Event Assistants Georgina Cassidy
and Martin Buchanan

CONTRIBUTORS features

it's been year for CREA standards

a cracking

TIVE

Until last year, our annual Design & Communication Awards had been a largely online affair. The live briefs that the awards centre on were purely published on the web, as was a showcase of the most outstanding submissions.

And then in 2003, we launched this book – an annual collaboration with John Brown Citrus Publishing where we could present the very latest live briefs alongside a showcase of the most outstanding work of the previous year, plus other contributions from creative professionals. book 03.04 was distributed nationwide, landing in the hands of students, tutors and industry figures. It provided people with something physical, something to take away with them, scribble on and be inspired by.

The number of submissions for this year's awards increased emphatically, and with greater quantity came arresting quality. I hope that, as you explore the pages of book 04.05, you will agree with all those in both rounds of judging that it's been a cracking year for creative standards.

Inevitably there's a finite number of pages in a book – which brings me back to the web. By the time you read this, our brand new website will be online. There you will find unlimited space for an extended showcase of the best of this year's awards, including all of the interactive and moving image work that couldn't be shown at its best in print.

It's also on the web that you'll find the core of our bold new recruitment initiative, ycn Creative Direction – an attempt to continually connect young creative talent with industry recruiters. Many thanks again to The Chase, London for the wonderful work in developing its visual identity.

This year's brand new collection of live creative challenges can be found at the other end of this book and we look forward again to bringing the very best work submitted to the attention of a huge creative audience.

Nick Defty
Director, ycn

last year's BRIEFS

The Sun: Create an integrated campaign designed to encourage students to read The Sun regularly. This is likely to be one main theme but adapted for different media.

Direct Line: Create TV advertising to get young people to call Direct Line first when they're getting a quote for motor insurance.

FT.com: Produce a design for the new interactive desktop news service that will be offered to FT.com subscribers.

Ginsters: Extend the Ginsters 'Real Honest Food' campaign to the point-of-sale environment.

Tetley: Encourage 18 to 24-year-olds to drink more tea.

Durex: Design packaging, on-pack graphics and point of sale for Durex condoms, specifically targeted at 16 to 24-year-olds.

Smile: Create an original outline application that will be circulated virally and raise the profile of smile.co.uk

Playboy Network: Create on-air branding and promotion to sell the Playboy Network's three channel brands to new subscribers.

Plantronics: Explore wearable technology and design a 'headset of the future', demonstrating a social or professional context in which it would be used.

Brylcreem: Come up with ideas to build Brylcreem's image and to communicate to young men that the brand is now a modern and relevant styling range - not just 'the red pot'. You may wish to focus on devising a new product or product range, rethink packaging or look at other marketing activities to grab the attention of the target market.

Milk Development Council:
Increase the appeal of milk to
primary school children aged 4 to
11 years old. You should make milk
fun while communicating its
nutritional benefits.

William Hill: Develop a
promotional campaign aimed at
motivating 18 to 35-year-olds to bet
on the 2004 European Football
Championships.

Smirnoff Ice: Smirnoff ice =
'smart'. It allows you to be the
person you are when you're on top
form, the guy everyone wants to be.
Communicate this in a way that will
appeal to leading-edge male
consumers. Think about the best
way to integrate this into the
market, and do so in any media
of your choosing.

National Aids Trust: Create a
communication strategy to increase
understanding among young adults
of the impact HIV-related stigma
and discrimination has on those
living with, affected by or presumed
to be HIV-positive.

Pot Noodle: Using ambient
communication, expose Pot Noodle
as a trashy, illicit pleasure.

Orange: Design and illustrate
new numbers for the Orange
Fair campaign.

John Brown Citrus Publishing:
Conceive a new magazine for 18 to
25-year-olds of both sexes.

Warbutons: Design on-pack
graphics and consider packaging
formats for Warburtons Milk Roll.
Your creative must achieve great
shelf stand-out and communicate
the goodness associated with the
product, while injecting an element
of fun that is relevant and appealing
to the ultimate consumer: kids.

Lexus: Launch Lexus Hybrid and
catapult Lexus to the forefront of
automotive technology again.

Michael Page International:
Challenge perceptions of what it is
to be a recruitment consultant and
inspire people to consider a career
with Michael Page International.

Ryan Dilley
ycn Username ryandilley
College University of
Gloucestershire
Course BA (Hons) Graphic
Design and Professional Media
Tutors Mike Abbey and
Vicky Baker

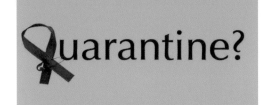

Dan Hedger
ycn Username neverland
College Somerset College of
Art and Technology
Course BA (Hons) Advertising
Tutor Stewart Owen

Michelle Ridge
Commended
ycn Username Michelle Ridge
College Norwich School
of Art and Design
Course BA (Hons)
Graphic Design
Tutor Vicki Winteringham

"Good use of paper, giving
a screen printed feel. Rather
tired subject but with strong,
confident graphics and
typography that make the
most of its lo-fi look and feel."
Jeremy Leslie,
Creative Director, JBCP

Matt Penberthy
ycn Usnername matt_p
College Hastings College
Course HND 2D-3D Design and
Communication
Tutors David Fowler and
Andrew Aloof

Marie Ronn
Stine Hole

Our favourite cartoon is Noggin the Nog. As members of the Scandinavian Society, we feel obligated to support our heritage. **We collect** garden gnomes. We started when we discovered that they were only £1 each at Holloway car boot sale. **Our normal tipple** is surgical spirit, which is cheap and effective. Be nice to your GP and he will be nice to you. **Daytime television** is the most underrated thing in the world. **The greatest artists of our age** are David Copperfield and Tarjei Bodin Larsen – an amazing new talent from the fjords of Norway. **The one sense we could live without** would be smell, which could be great on the tube and when entering public toilets. **Our worst vice** is going to view expensive flats, saying we'll take them. Just for fun.

Stine and Marie's work is on page 104

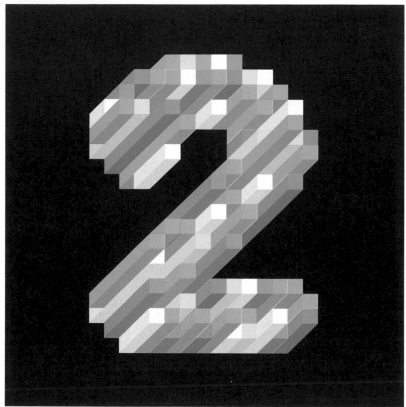

Tom Lane
ycn Username
therealgingerprince
College University of the
West of England
Course BA (Hons) Graphic
Communication
Tutors Rob Kettel and
Sam Deeks

Dominic Witter
Commended
ycn Username Witter
College Liverpool John
Moores University
Course BA (Hons) Graphic Arts
Tutor John Young
Award £50 pool allocation

Sarah Pidgeon
ycn Username Pidgeon
College Norwich School of
Art and Design
Course BA (Hons) Graphic
Design
Tutor Ray Gregory

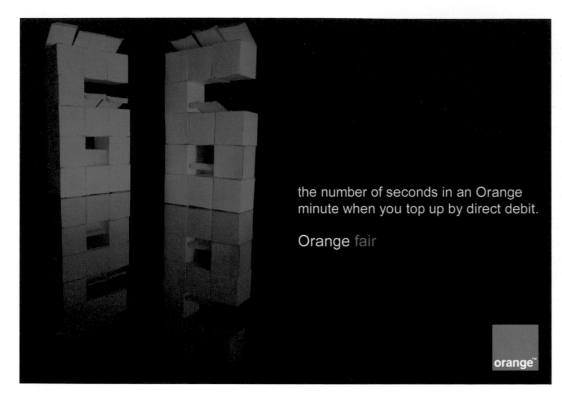

the number of seconds in an Orange
minute when you top up by direct debit.

Orange fair

orange™

Free reverse calls
when you run out of
credit.

Orange fair

Subject to status.

Orange

Katharine Louise Garnett
Commended
ycn Username katharine
College Glasgow School of Art
Course BA (Hons) Visual
Communication
Tutors Sophie Morrish
Award £50 pool allocation

"A believable, ownable and
great idea." Jon Edge, Design
Director, Interbrand

Sean Lingwood
ycn Username seanlingwood
College Bath Spa
University College
Course BA (Hons) Graphic
Design
Tutors David Beaugeard,
Paul Minott, Jack Gardner

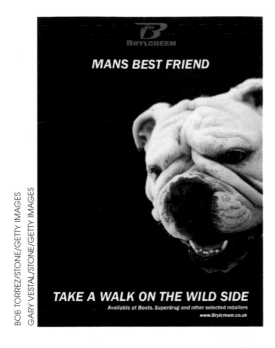

BOB TORREZ/STONE/GETTY IMAGES
GARY VESTAL/STONE/GETTY IMAGES

Daniel Welch
Commended
ycn Username welcdj
College Falmouth College
of Arts
Course BA (Hons) Graphic
Design
Tutor Mafalda Spencer
Award £500 pool allocation

"Well thought-out packaging
demonstrating a sound
understanding of core
Brylcreem cues. Excellent
presentation and explanation
of thought process."
Andy Rawle, Brand Manager,
Brylcreem

feature
12 months in DESIGN

Here are the most stand-out designs of the last 12 months, in the order that they occur to me.

August 03 Ship of Ideas: Atelier Markgraph

At nightfall each evening during Frankfurt's 2003 Museum Bank Festival, a floating, illuminated cube consisting of projection screens and LEDs glided along the River Main. As it passed, it offered glimpses of the exhibitions on show along the river bank – the display changing as it passed each one. This *Ship of Ideas* deservedly won a D&AD Gold this year – a classic case of "I wish I'd thought of that". How about an airship version floating over London? You could text messages to it, get it to point you in the right direction if you were lost, maybe you could even get it to lead your dodgy mini-cab driver home so there'd be no more rows about his "special short-cuts".

Opened Summer 03 JR Tower Sapporo: Studio Compasso

Another D&AD winner, and another great use of the environment. At the top of the JR Tower in Sapporo, Japan, is an observatory. Normally what happens in these things is a lot of pointing and arguing along the following lines: "Where's such and such then?", "Is that north?", "Can you see my house?". Studio Compasso came up with a stunning solution. The tower is next to a main railway station so the designers

decided to use its roof as their map. Giant type with directional arrows point out all the local places of interest to observatory viewers above.

April 04 Photographs of torture from Abu Ghraib prison

The abiding image of the Iraq war will not be one provided by a professional photojournalist, but will be the hooded prisoner standing on a box, snapped by an unknown prison guard. Now we can all be photojournalists, unwittingly or not. It is now almost impossible to control the outflow of images from the world's conflict zones. What's the point of banning cameramen when your own soldiers are busy snapping away? This would seem, on the face of it, to be a good thing: censorship is no longer as easily enforceable. But there's a problem, as the *Daily Mirror* found to its cost, the provenance of such images is always going to be uncertain. The photojournalist may not have the same access as these visual whistleblowers, but he or she does operate with an integrity that gives us faith in their work, despite the mutability of the digital image.

Until Sept 03 The Peter Saville Show

Graphic design may be all around us but, to the general public, it is all but invisible. This is partly because the national media have virtually no interest in graphic design. Architecture, advertising, product and furniture design are all regularly featured in the national press but never graphics. Until last year. The Design Museum's Peter Saville Show finally broke through with abundant coverage in the broadsheets (as we could then still call them). You can see the attraction for the feature's editor with pages to fill. Firstly, Saville is the king of record sleeves, which are accessible and understandable. Secondly, because he does record sleeves, he's got lots of famous and glamourous friends from that world and from his other great sphere of influence – fashion. And thirdly, because he is Peter Saville – hugely charismatic, perpetually in crisis, extremely intelligent and eloquent, and just about the most astute cultural commentator that design has. Finally, some public recognition of what design does.

From May 03 Honda Cog: Wieden + Kennedy

Undoubtedly the most talked-about commercial of last year. Gavin Lucas, our staff writer, came back from The Mill raving about a new ad that he'd just been shown. We got a tape in – it was amazing and we decided to do a story on how it was made. But. hang on, doesn't it look like that art film where all this stuff sets off chain reactions? My problem with *Cog* is not that an advert has taken "inspiration" from fine art – that happens all the time (did you know, for example, that the Silk Cut campaign was based on the slash paintings of Lucio Fontana, several of which were owned by Charles Saatchi?). My problem is that, by referencing Fischli and Weiss' *Der Lauf Der Dinge* so closely, the makers of *Cog* took away the right of the artists to do what they want with their own work. They can never show that piece again without people thinking of Honda. Two years ago, Mark Romanek made a video for the Red Hot Chili Peppers' *Can't Stop*. It was based on the *One Minute Sculptures* of Austrian artist, Erwin Wurm. The end frame

explained the video was inspired by Wurm, encouraging a new audience to seek out his work. How much more elegant would it have been if *Cog* had done the same?

February 04 Hype: Publicis

Some day, all ad campaigns may be made this way. Hewlett Packard and their agency, Publicis, had a very straightforward goal. They wanted to promote HP kit – printers, projectors etc – to a young, creative audience, and to establish a relationship with them. Publicis could have simply suggested ads in the design press, perhaps run a competition with a printer as a prize. Instead they came up with a project that is a great illustration of the new thinking in advertising. Publicis hired a gallery space in Brick Lane. But they had nothing to put in it. Instead, the gallery opened completely empty. Imagemakers were encouraged to bring along their work on disc, where it was printed out or projected on HP kit *in situ* and put up on the walls. Everyone was welcome, no-one was turned away. The result: a living, growing exhibition that changed every day as new work went up and old work came down.

September 03 The Independent goes tabloid

The story: failing broadsheet goes tabloid and shakes up European newspaper industry. A number of British broadsheet newspapers had been considering switching to tabloid format for years – rumour has it that most have a tabloid paper ready-designed and locked away in a vault. But *The Independent*, beset by commercial problems, took the plunge first. It had to. And it worked – after its switch to tabloid, *The Independent*'s circulation went up by 25 per cent. The effect was incredible. Almost immediately, *The Times* followed suit. Stories were rife that, as soon as its ownership was sorted out, the *Daily Telegraph* would be next. Now *The Guardian* has admitted that it will be swapping to the *Berliner* format. The tabloid stigma had been shaken off – downsizing did not equal downmarket. But should we be pleased or horrified that the mini-*Indy*'s success has been achieved largely in spite of its editorial design? The tabloid is simply a squashed version of the broadsheet. It's too dense and, at times, downright ugly. But the format is so strong readers love it anyway. A "proper" redesign is in the works but the size is what matters.

November 03 The Director's Label DVDs

Directing pop promos was always seen as a handy stepping stone to bigger, and, it was presumed, better things – feature films. Music videos were ephemeral, flitting across MTV for the life of the single before disappearing from whence they came. But video compilations and the explosion in the number of music TV channels has given the promo longevity. And its ubiquity has led to an unexpected level of interest in promo directors, helped, no doubt, by the fact that some channels identify them in the credits at the end of the video. So now we have The Director's Label – a line of DVD compilations by leading music video directors marketed not to fans of the bands but to fans of the directors themselves. The first three to be released are *Spike Jonze*, *Michel Gondry* and *Chris Cunningham*. The label was Jonze's idea as he wanted to gather

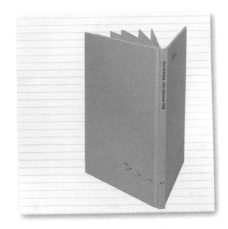

his diverse back catalogue in one place. Recognising that Gondry and Cunningham were of similar calibre, he suggested they set up a label and make their compilations its first three releases. We've had star designers (well, stars in their own little universe) for years, complete with lavish monographs, eagerly anticipated public appearances and ardent fans – now music video directors are attracting similar adoration.

October 03 Fifth Rencontres de la Photographie Africaine

In 1996, curator André Magnin saw the work of an anonymous African photographer in an exhibition in New York. So taken was he by these studio portraits of local people in their Sunday best, posing with whatever object meant most to them (however unlikely) that he decided to seek out the artist. In Bamako, the capital of the west-African state of Mali, Magnin found his man. A local camera repair store owner identified the work as that of Seydou Keïta. Magnin went on to edit the first

monograph of Keïta's images, published by Scalo in 1997. Keïta went on to exhibit and work internationally: Fabien Baron commissioned him to shoot a *Harper's Bazaar* fashion story while Janet Jackson's *Got Till It's Gone* promo was based on his pictures. Keïta opened the world's eyes to African photography. The Rencontres de la Photographie Africaine, staged every other year in Bamako, Mali, proves that there are plenty more where he came from. This year's festival featured work from all over Africa addressing the theme of the sacred and the profane. The top prize (the Seydou Keïta Award) went to Egyptian Youssef Nabil for a series of exquisite, hand-tinted portraits. Other notable work included a retrospective section traced the history of photography in Africa.

July to December 03 Fourth Estate catalogue: Tom Hingston Studio

Just a beautiful object. Fourth Estate is a small publisher with a history of fine design collaborations – Vince Frost used to do its catalogues. Somewhat symbolically, the baton has now passed to Tom Hingston (many people's choice as heir apparent to the title of leading graphic designer) but the quality remains. Drawing its inspiration from the idea of an author's manuscript, ASCII characters are used to illustrate a selection of works offered in the July-December 2003 catalogue while titles, blurb and review extracts are all set in a simple typewriter font. I have no intention of buying any Fourth Estate books but I treasure this catalogue.

Patrick Burgoyne is editor of Creative Review

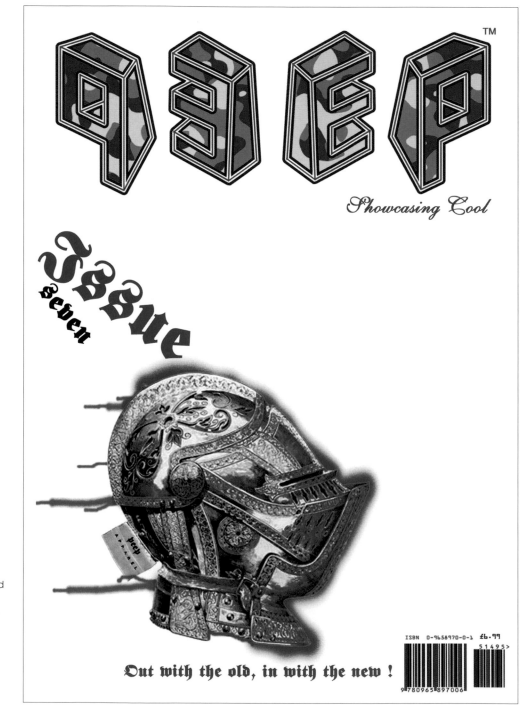

Michael D Clague
Commended
ycn Username dclague
College UWIC
Course BA (Hons) Graphic
Communication
Tutor Ray Nicklin

"It was the cover that attracted
us to this entry, the logo in
particular. The insides were less
convincing as editorial design
but had an energy and
difference to the other entries
that helped us decide to
include it here." Jeremy Leslie,
Creative Director, JBCP

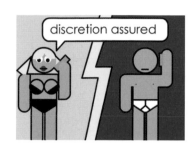

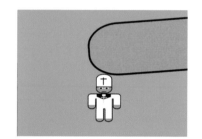

**Tom Rayment
Adam Sullivan
Commended
ycn Username** Raymentski
College Camberwell
College of Arts
Course BA (Hons) Graphic
Design
Tutor Patrick Roberts
Award £1000 pool allocation

"A great effort and a totally refreshing approach to adult entertainment TV. It had the office in hysterics! It was original and even though a lot of the humour was clichéd (which we usually tend to avoid), we felt that in a cartoon format it was actually very effective. This work would enable people to talk about adult entertainment in a public forum without any embarrassment, and also had good PR potential. The promo was obviously aimed towards male viewers but also had the potential to be appreciated by by women and certainly not be found offensive. As someone who has worked in the adult entertainment business for more than four years, it was refreshing to see some creative that didn't consist of girls in bikinis talking seductively to camera. We did feel however that the work was let down a little by the on-screen subscription messages which were slightly unclear. The delivery of the ordering information is obviously vital."
Richard Gale,
Head of European
Marketing, Playboy TV

**Also commended for
Playboy TV
Matthew Brannick**
Manchester Metropolitan
University
**Matthew's work can be seen
at www.ycnonline.com**

Dean Pannifer
Commended
ycn Username Pannifer
College Glasgow School of Art
Course BA (Hons) Visual
Communication
Tutors Steve Rigley, Joe Petty
and Brian Cairns
Award Rocket, £400 pool
allocation and creative
placement at JKR

"Everyone loved the tea-stains
graphics. So simple but yet so
visually strong and with such a
natural feel."
Nick Kilby, Head of Marketing,
Tetley

Neville Brody

My favourite dinosaur is vinyl, because you can't beat that sound. **I want my last words** to be 'See you again'. **I would hire** Le Corbusier to redecorate my house. **The best invention in history** is peace. Because it's peace. **I prefer** lakes to beaches, for the stillness and solitude. **If I could redesign anything**, it would be global debt. **Evil on its own** does not exist. We are all co-conspirators.

Neville Brody is co-founder of Research Studios

**Jonathan Tran and
Kwok Fung Lam
ycn Usernames** thetranny
and kwoksta

"Very few entrants managed
to produce something that
covered the entire age range.
This piece was wonderfully
animated but seemed to
directly appeal to the younger
part of the target market."
Philippa Stagg, Milk
Development Council

Philip Postill
ycn Username phil postill
College Lincoln University
Course BA (Hons) Graphic
Design

"HUH"

"MUH"

"BIG ELVIS"

"THE LEADER"

Yasuko Nakama
Commended
ycn Username yasuko
College City College
Manchester
Course HND Graphic Design
Tutor Joanne Greenhaulgh
Award £100 pool allocation

"Excellent overall concept and
great slogan. Designs felt a little
cluttered but very distinctive in
style." Philippa Stagg, Milk
Development Council

Matthew Smith
Commended
ycn Username m_smith
College Hull School of Art
and Design
Course HND Graphic Design
Tutors Phillipa Wood and
Chris Dunn
Award £250 pool allocation

"Innovative idea for the
masthead (reflecting the
magazine's concept), raw
contemporary design style
throughout and an unfinished
look made it refreshingly
different from all the highly
finished Quark layouts we saw.
Had a young, energetic retro
look without being too kitsch."
Jeremy Leslie, Creative
Director, JBCP

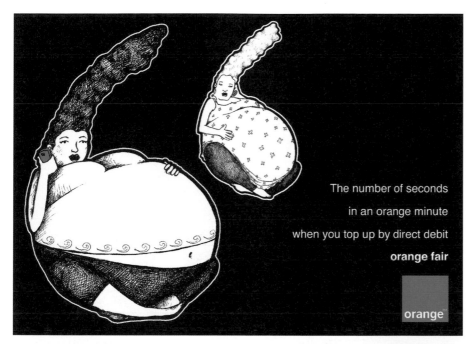

The number of seconds
in an orange minute
when you top up by direct debit
orange fair

orange

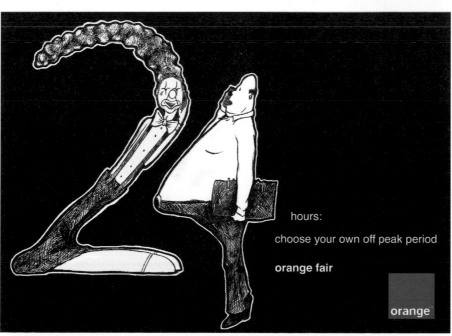

hours:
choose your own off peak period
orange fair

orange

Zandra Rolfe
Commended
ycn Username zandra
College University College
Northampton
Course BA (Hons) Graphic
Communication
Tutor Barry Wenden
Award £50 pool allocation

Also commended for Orange
Shaun Rayner
Amersham and Wycombe
College
Shaun's work can be seen at
www.ycnonline.com

Steven Croft
Commended
ycn Username stevec
College Northbrook
College, Sussex
Course BA (Hons)
Communication Design
Tutor Priscilla McIntosh
Award £100 pool allocation

"Strong designs, great vending
concepts although soya and
goat's milk were off brief."
Philippa Stagg, Milk
Development Council

Jonathan Silcock
Commended
Award £750 pool allocation
and possible placement
at HHCL Red Cell

"Curtain brilliantly takes the idea
of filth and illicit temptation in
store. Very funny, on brand and
who wouldn't be able to resist
having a look. Very brave and
confident to cover up your
brand at point of purchase."
Andy Davis, HHCL Red Cell

Sylvie Barr

I like circles because they're everywhere in nature, from our planet to our body cells. I also like squares because they're about structure.
My favourite building is Battersea Power Station – I see it every morning. I wish it were being looked after like the Tate Modern. **I relax** in my garden, as I find gardening quite therapeutic – it's so satisfying to watch your plants and flowers grow from just a few little seeds. **My worst habit** is faffing in the morning when I need to get ready to go on a trip, and the train or plane won't wait for me. **If there's one song** I can listen to again and again, it's *Mon Amie La Rose*. It's an old French song, recently remixed by Natacha Atlas, about how ephemeral life is. **The best thing I ever bought** was my house. Buying early in your adult life is quite a British thing and being French, it took me a while to take the plunge.

Sylvie Barr is Head of Marketing at Cafédirect

The people from **Milk Land** drink milk every day because it helps them live fit and healthy lives. It is very good for keeping their teeth and bones strong.

Jacob Vanderkar
ycn Username jacob
College Bath Spa
University College
Course BA (Hons)
Graphic Design
Tutors David Beaugeard,
Paul Minott, Jack Gardner

Rachel Mountifield
ycn Username crazeybrit
College Bath Spa University
College
Course BA (Hons)
Graphic Design
Tutors David Beaugeard, Paul
Minott, Jack Gardner

Position No.15 - Hot Poodle

Position No.12 - Meal For 2

Position No.09 - Smoky Bacon

Position No.17 - The Snatch

Thomas Bradley
Commended
ycn Username Bradley
College Hull School of
Art and Design
Course BA (Hons)
Graphic Design
Tutors Alex Rabone

"Irreverent, shocking, filthy
and funny." Andy Davis,
HHCL Red Cell

O····· front cover

O dummy

content page O·····

Gloria Lew Cheek Ning
Commended
ycn Username BB01982
College Manchester
Metropolitan University
Course BA (Hons) Design
and Art Direction
Tutor Lenore Gristwood

"Strong concept with a
powerful cover displaying the
beginnings of a bright, exciting
execution targeting its
audience well. Let down by
some of the page designs –
particularly the contents page."
Jeremy Leslie, Creative
Director, JBCP

Steve Johnston

My earliest memories are: big orange space hopper, sun, Action Man. **My favourite shop** is a restaurant called "Tai Terrific" in Bondi, which serves the best seafood curry. **I'll share a coffee** with anyone, you get much better conversations from random people. **I admire** Carling, how can you not buy into a brand that helps you feel so good? Makes you fall over though. **The first name in my mobile phone** is Amie, a mate of my girlfriend's. She's got really long nails and likes to bite guys. **My favourite joke** is 'What do you call a man with a seagull on his head?' **I can't really think** of any big mistakes I've done. Lots of things I should have done, I regret those more. **You never know** when you need to quickly identify a designer, on the street, at the beach. That's why they all wear black – so that you know they mean business.

Steve Johnston is director of the Phantom Research Foundation

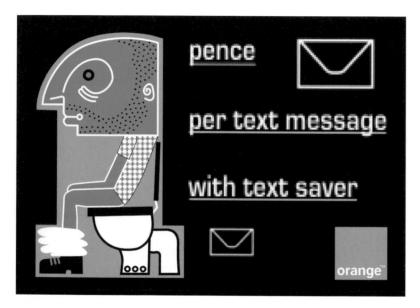

Johnathon Grimwood
Commended
ycn Username grimmers
College Loughborough
University School of Art
and Design
Course BA (Hons) Visual
Communication (Illustration)
Tutor Andrew Selby
Award £50 pool allocation

Also commended for Orange
Nicholas Butterfield
University of Gloucestershire
Nicholas' work can be seen
at www.ycnonline.com

Marketa Cooper
ycn Username Marketa
College University of
Gloucestershire
Course BA (Hons) Graphic
Design and Professional Media
Tutors Mike Abbey and
Vicky Baker

Sam McCullen
Commended
ycn Username sam79
College Cambridge
School of Art –APU
Course MA Childrens
Book Illustration
Tutor Martin Salisbury
Award Rocket and
£600 pool allocation

"Loved it! Informative, funny,
exciting. Hits all the ages in just
the right way. A wonderful
piece of work." Philippa Stagg,
Milk Development Council

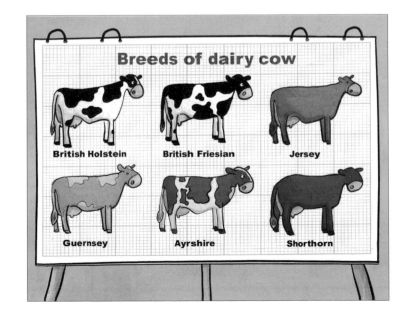

feature

how to b

INVISIBLE

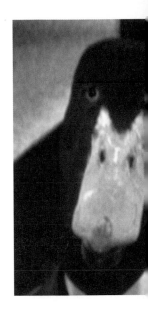

Face up to the truth

A lot of people believe that creatives have lost the plot. Nowadays it's not about the brief, the customer, the client. It's all about the mantlepiece. As ex-copywriter Frederic Beigbeder puts it, "A good copywriter never targets the consumer but the 20 people most likely to employ him (the creative directors of the 20 best advertising agencies). Consequently, winning prizes at Cannes or at the CD& AD Club is far more important than winning market share for a client."

The words appear in his novel £9.99, about life in a fictional ad agency. But in mid 2004, Beigbeder's cynical insights crossed over into the real world. *Campaign* ran a story about the new managing director of Nestlé Rowntree UK, Chris White. On taking over, White immediately struck a blow on behalf of long-suffering clients. White believed the company's previous advertising for products such as Kit Kat were no good. "I don't like any of the ads," he said. "They are focussed on awards and not on selling more product to more people, at higher prices."

A moment of transparent honesty. White nailed creative indulgence, and delivered a direct, uncomplicated, version of what advertising should be about – selling more product at higher prices. The message is that creatives have lost their intellectual discipline. Like brattish kids indulged for too long, creatives may be losing their sense of responsibility for the client or the job.

Remember: no-one gives a monkey's

Most creatives, ironically especially award-winning ones, would not disagree with the sentiment. "The public don't really give a monkey's about advertising," says Matt Gooden, Art Director on Wieden & Kennedy's *Everyday* for Honda.

Gooden has won awards, famously for *Cog* and again more recently for *Everyday*. These are outstandingly eye-catching ads, portfolio pieces that will open doors, pull up a chair and slip a vodka martini into any prospective client's hand. But the ads can be sourced back to basic requirements of the client. *Everyday* as a creative spot would not have worked for just any car. "If BMW had done it," says Gooden, "it would have been a lot darker and a lot colder, not so emotional. Lots of cold metal shot quite moodily."

Practical can be fun

Honda is not a moody brand. It's more human and optimistic than BMW's engineering futurism. "The Honda Civic is an amazingly functional car", says Gooden. "They've thought about every part of it. The brief was to make the practical appealing. 'Practical' is quite a boring sort of brief."

But 'practical' is the bread and butter of advertising. In product advertising, as opposed to brand advertising, it's more often than not about the practical. It is the most transparent form of advertising appeal – buy this because it does that. Gooden and his colleague Ben Walker packaged the practical around technologies of everyday life.

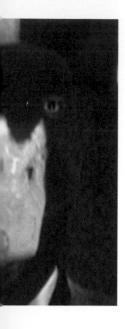

As you watch, you tick off each item, 'alarm, toothbrush, tap, flush, zip, sliced bread, toaster, kettle, teabag, flip-top bin.' The viewing pleasure is the anticipation of what you already know. Your mental space is immediately organised; you know what you are going to see and still enjoy it. Which is how Gooden and Walker turned the concept of 'the practical' into a psychological experience, wrapping it all up with the pay-off "Why is it, the better something does its job, the more you take it for granted?".

Don't add. Subtract

With every execution, the creativity lies not in the addition but in the subtraction. What you take out is worth more than what you put in. The kinds of creative indulgence that Chris White fumes at can often happen when the execution loses a sense of what drove it in the first place. Gooden explains, "When we cut together everything [on *Everyday*], there was a lot more stuff in there. One of our Creative Directors said: 'I'm not looking at this film until you're happy with it. It's very difficult to judge work when you get close to it.' Then he found it very easy. He said: 'Look, it's getting far too complicated.'" Award-winning work and delivering to the client is all about the edit. "You do have to pull things back a lot," Gooden says.

What you should pull things back to is something that allows the brand tone of voice to be heard and seen without ambiguity. The advertising communication shouldn't get in the

way – the creative becomes invisible. And the reason Gooden's spot works for the client is the one necessary ingredient of all great creative. It's there in Honda's strapline. "Why is it, the better something does its job, the more you take it for granted?" With great creative, you just don't notice it.

Do the right thing in the right place at the right time

The age of creativity for creativity's sake is history. At least that's the view of TBWA's Bil Bungay: "The worst kind of creativity is profligate creativity: taking the client's cash and trying to write an ad that will further your own career, that's going to win awards, in complete ignorance and denial of client objectives. I think creatives like that are gradually becoming obsolete. Advertising agencies have to be successful."

Bungay has worked with colleague Trevor Beattie on the French Connection and the Playstation campaigns. Keeping on message, connecting back to the client, product or brand, not pursuing a fanciful idea requires the creative to "be the best door-to-door salesman out there", says Bungay. There are four essential items that will guarantee at least the possibility of getting the communication right. "They should know exactly what to say, in the right way, to the right audience, at the right time." That's how to turn invisible.

Develop the hunch

The problem with creativity for creativity's sake is that it builds an inconsistent communication around the product or brand. You have to intimately know the brand you are communicating. "You develop an instinct," says Bungay. "You train it, hone it, learn about an environment, learn about your

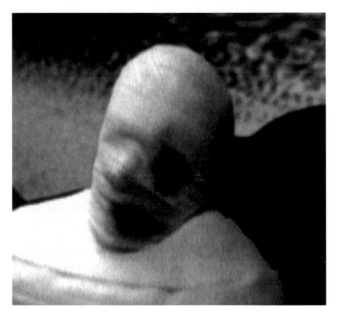

audience. A detective might call it a hunch. A hunch is an understanding of your environment so comprehensive that you can process all of the information in a subconscious way and sense there is a right way of doing something."

The hunch becomes your filter. Says Bungay, "It's your perception of what's going on in the field of advertising, what's going on in terms of consumerism, the mood of a nation… all the subtleties that everyone absorbs around them."

Create the language

The PlayStation ads are among the most transparent ads around. Bungay and his colleagues and client have given the PlayStation its own advertising language of 'The Third Place'. It's a prime example of what happens when the creative instinct finds the vocabulary to match. Transparency isn't about clarity. It's about finding the tone of voice that can only belong to one product or brand. It's the visual DNA of the brand that those who need to know will recognise. As Bungay says, "Pretty much all the commercials we've ever done for PlayStation your mum won't have seen. Clearly she's not the audience. If by some miracle she saw one, she is so not going to get it."

The PlayStation ads have such a unique tone and visual vocabulary that your mother might not even have registered them. Like being abroad and hearing a language you don't understand, it just washes over you. The TBWA ads have given a language to The Third Place, a place that exists in a different perceptual plane for those receptive to a visit.

Deliver the ESP

"I like to talk about this thing called an ESP," says Bungay. "An emotional selling point. We used to have Unique Selling Point, but I prefer to think of an ESP that a product has to offer. People buy into an emotional connection with a product."

But it's difficult to get right. PlayStation ads don't talk about its processing power, its memory or anything at all to do with function. Bungay, Beattie and the client worked together to conceptualise the ESP of the PlayStation, The Third Place. "The first place is home, the second place is work, The Third Place is your PlayStation," says Bungay. "When Trevor and I launched PlayStation 2, we had David Lynch make a film for us. It's still my favourite film. It's utterly timeless. Tonally it's just so right, taking so many risks with what you can and can't do. It is a beautiful representation of the Third Place."

Find a Big Idea

The Third Place is a Big Idea. If you have a Big Idea in your communications, your execution will be invisible. A Big Idea is a concept that runs everything, that everything maps back to, whether you work on brand marketing or hard selling.

The concept emerged out of the advertising revolution of the 1960s. It allowed advertising to move away from the psychologically static communications of the 1950s, and to compete with the dynamic visual culture of the age.

Ads designed solely to win awards, by definition do not have a Big Idea. A Big Idea gives the rationale for every part of the campaign and is the filter through which every individual idea has to pass. An advert with a Big Idea changes the space it launches into. It changes the language of the culture.

What The Third Place had as a Big Idea was to take a piece of computer hardware and turn it into a belief system. The PlayStation "is much bigger than video games" says Bungay. "It's a way of life. It's the Third Place. It's living, breathing. If all you are is work routine and home routine, you are missing out on what you as a human being are capable of experiencing. Go and climb, jump off a mountain, that's a real experience. PlayStation offers you experiences like these, as close as you can without hurting yourself. Come and live the experience."

If the focus for the designer is just to win awards then they'd do well to listen to the words of Adrian Shaughnessy, a freelance creative and frequent D&AD judge. "I think the market for design has hardened in recent years," he says. "Clients are fixated on results – which is another way of saying they want effectiveness. So they will only support work that is, in their view, effective. This makes it harder to do original and innovative work. When 'effectiveness' becomes the sole benchmark you tend to lose risk and surprise.

"But it is only immature designers who don't want their work to be 'effective'. Pleasing yourself is important – it's why most of us become designers. But you won't last long if you only ever think about pleasing yourself. You have to combine it with doing striking and original work that is effective. That's the trick, and all the really great designers do both."

Know nothing

Sometimes knowing little about your product is the best starting point. Simon Brown along with John Link from Tomorrow London designed a publishing project for architect and maverick Rem Koolhaas and his company OMA. The pair weren't familiar with the culture of architects. The brief according to Brown was "to create an architectural magazine that was affordable and accessible to non-architects". The result was *Content*, a fabulous, mad wedge of informative material and ideas rendered in what Brown calls "a mook", a cross between a book and a magazine.

To be as transparent to as wide a number of people as possible, Brown and Link ignored the conventions of architecture and design magazines (white space) and took their reference points form Dutch gay and lesbian porn magazines and Japanese and Chinese catalogues. We are used to seeing perfectly packaged communications with little to say, so *Content* is as visually provocative as the words within that speak of anti-globalisation and protest. It's not that it looks random, because it isn't. It looks 'default'. It looks punk. All our communications – advertising, newspapers, magazines – are so carefully staged, manicured, pampered, for fear of introducing anything a little too brittle, that the content itself is neutralised.

This is why the design of *Content* is so refreshing, and why it is one of the best communications of 2004. It appears so full of information and images that it makes understanding and being informed seem 'hot'. Which is what OMA and Koolhaas communicate as a brand. Those who ask Koolhaas and his team to pitch for commissions aren't just buying a building – they buy an unconventional philosophy of 21st-century space.

contents

The design was helped by the fact that Brown and Link didn't have an architectural background. They didn't treat Koolhaas as a guru. Brown explains, "We had no previous connection to him, which was a nice way to work. It means you work with ideas that you, and so an average person, can understand."

Being invisible sometimes means being fresh.

Know everything

If *Content* succeeded because its creatives had a lack of history, *Bollocks* for Volkswagen succeeded because of its history. A little girl has a series of mishaps, such as dropping her ice-cream, and exclaims "Bollocks!". The narrative is told in reverse, so you are kept in suspense until the final frame when the dad holding a petrol pump exclaims "Bollocks!". The strapline is "Don't forget it's a diesel." What's interesting about this ad is the swearing. Conventionally, it's a cheap trick to get attention. Amber Casey, who created the ad with Dan Hubert for BMP DDB, argues, "It wasn't using swearing only for sensationalist purposes. It really expressed a truth." The history of provocative VW ads allows such executions to sit comfortably with the brand.

Bollocks is intended to generate the VW ad experience of an "intelligent, inside smile as a payoff", says Casey. "It's where you are rewarding yourself for getting the gag. And whatever that gag is, it's related to a strategic thought, to a strong message."

Be honest

Being invisible is about being honest. It's about delivering the appropriate communication, in the right way at the right time, as Bil Bungay says. Some argue that you must value effectiveness over creativity. But it's a false conflict. As Adrian Shaugnessy says, great creativity is effective.

In his book *$ellebrity*, the great Art Director George Lois defines creativity as "one per cent inspiration, nine per cent perspiration and 90 per cent justification. Selling and protecting your work (to those around you, to lawyers, to TV copy clearance, and to your client) is what separates the sometimes good creative from the consistently great one". Creativity, as Bil Bungay said, is about being able to sell your idea to clients who will believe in and support your work. It's not easy. Everyone has their own agendas, even those representing a client. Agreeing with the client at all times may be the path of least resistance, but individuals in corporations protect their own interests as much as everyone else. Through experience, you learn which are the battles worth fighting. Advertising emerges out of all those messy human relationships.

When you leave college, giving up creativity for its own sake isn't easy. Being invisible is about creating honest communication. If that becomes too difficult, write a list of the key points you're trying to convey. At least it makes it look as if you have remembered what the client asked you to do in the first place. At least it gives the impression of transparency. And then just hope that they don't see right through you.
John O'Reilly is the editor of Edit magazine

Katerina Lendacka
Commended
ycn Username kat lendacka
College University College
Northampton
Course BA (Hons) Graphic
Communication
Tutor Barry Wenden
Award £50 pool allocation

Manish Patel
ycn Username manishpatel
College University College
Northampton
Course BA (Hons) Graphic
Communication
Tutors Paul Wilson and
Barry Wenden

Michael Lloyd
Commended
ycn Username M_J_LLOYD_1
College Blackburn College
Course BA (Hons)
Graphic Design
Tutor Helen Mathers
Award £500 pool allocation and
creative placement at DJPA

"The headline and sub headline worked very well together, both to support the image and to generate a call to action – this was helped further by consideration of the web/phone/shop message informing consumers how they could place a bet. The opportunity was missed though to show the football fans in a place other than just in front of the TV." Mark Saxby, Poulter Partners

Also commended for
William Hill
Paul Telling
Bath Spa University College
Mark Daw and
Gavin Tochet
Buckinghamshire Chilterns
University College
Phil Tait
University of Lincoln
Their work can be seen
at www.ycnonline.com

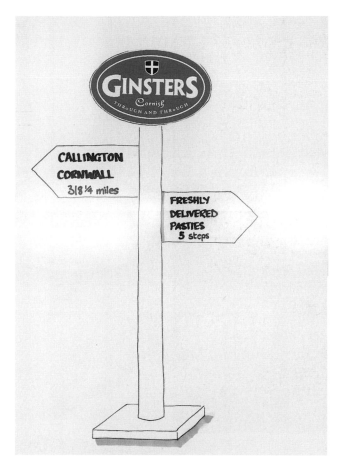

**Naomi Nicklin and
Thomas Chailand
Commended
ycn Username** nomienick
College Falmouth
College of Arts
Course PGDIP
Creative Advertising
Tutors Alice Taylor and
Digby Atkinson
Award £250 pool allocation

"The idea of placing the
communication within
the environment of fresh
vegetables was spot on, as
was the conveyor belt media
idea." Larry File, Marketing
Manager, Ginsters

**Also commended for Ginsters
Matt Underwood**
University of Derby
**George Salt and
Jennifer Farrington**
Falmouth College of Arts
**Warren Frost
Their work can be seen
at www.ycnonline.com**

Petrina Bec Ying Jones
Commended
ycn Username tree
College University of
Glamorgan
Course BA (Hons) Graphic
Communications
Tutor Gerald Emanuel
Award Rocket, £1000
pool allocation and
creative placement at DJPA

"This design demonstrated
strong clarity of thinking and
excellent execution which
would appeal to both Mum
and the kids, while answering
all aspects of the brief." Lesley
Wallwork, Marketing Manager,
Warburtons

Kwog Fung Lam
Jonathan Tran

K: **My first ever computer** was an Amiga 500. I remember having to constantly swap disks to load up a level in the middle of a game. **The best thing I can cook** is my BBQ chicken. It helped me win Master Chef '94. **When I was growing up** I wanted to be an animator/cartoonist. It was Rolf Harris' Cartoon Club that did it for me.

J: **The worst purchase** I ever made was a pair of lime-flared trousers that cost me a small fortune. **When I'm thinking**, I always doodle spheres. It stems from having silly competitions at school. **My favourite animals** are giraffes and salmon. **When I was a child**, I had a fear of ghosts. I would always have my eyes shut when I was in the dark, to prevent me from ever seeing one.

Kwok and Jonathan's work is on page 29

Rachel Mountfield
Commended
ycn Username crazeybrit
College Bath Spa
University College
Course BA (Hons)
Graphic Design
Tutor Paul Minott
Award £100 pool allocation

"Good strong designs and
an excellent message."
Philippa Stagg, Milk
Development Council

Peter Rapley
Commended
ycn Username raps
College Surrey Institute of Art
and Design University College
Course BA (Hons)
Packaging Design
Tutors Catherine Slade-Brooking
and Jack Blake
Award £300 pool allocation

"Idea seemed a little familiar
but this work was wonderfully
executed. We particulalry liked
extras such as the tray and felt
that this was an excellent
response to the brief."
Philippa Stagg, Milk
Development Council

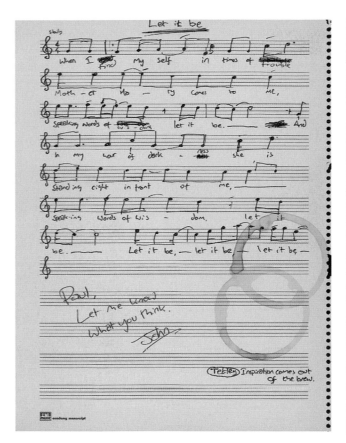

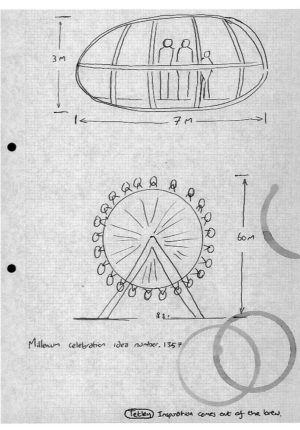

John Barron and
Jasper Colliver
Commended
ycn Username baz
Award £350 pool allocation

"We loved the simplicity of the creative idea. This is highly campaignable although perhaps not entirely targeted at younger consumers." Nick Kilby, Head of Marketing, Tetley

Also commended for Tetley
Sarah Warwick
University of Derby
Fraser Gordon
Napier University
Daniel Bond
University of Portsmouth
Philip Mewse
Surrey Institute of Art and Design
Evelyn Lehrer
University of Westminster
Their work can be seen
at www.ycnonline.com

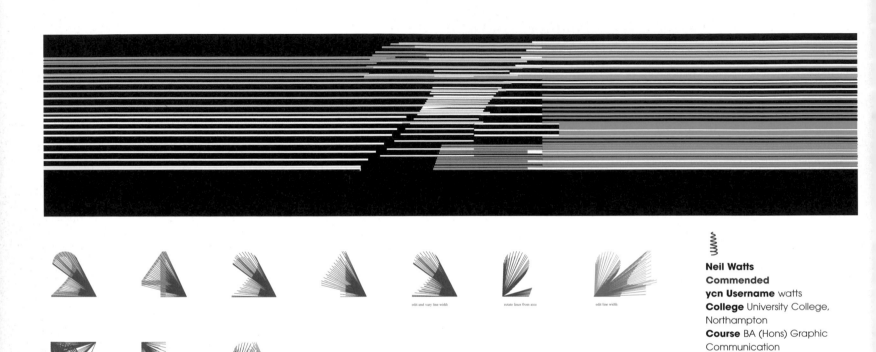

edit and vary line width

rotate lines from axis

edit line width

rotate around axis and layer

Neil Watts
Commended
ycn Username watts
College University College,
Northampton
Course BA (Hons) Graphic
Communication
Tutor Barry Wenden
Award Rocket and
£200 pool allocation

"We were really impressed
by this work, its sympathetic
presentation, systematic working
method, speculation of ideas
and range of outcomes. A
fascinating body of personal
and contemporary work."
Marie O'Connor and
Andrew Rae, Peepshow

Malcolm Jobling

I scan through lots of different newspapers in the course of the week, looking for the unusual and amusing stories – but I don't read the cartoons. **My most comfortable shoes** are my Brasher climbing boots. They look heavy and clumsy, but actually slip on like a glove and are totally waterproof and indestructible. **My favourite type of weather** changes with my mood. **I like being near the coast** when there's a warm, gentle breeze and I also like the excitement of thunder and lightning. I hate sitting still in the sun. **My desk** might contain anything from hub caps and bacon sandwiches to students' work and gallery information – all covered in reams of educational paperwork. **The best place in the country** is the top of Tryfan in North Wales. The top is quite small, but even in poor weather it is a peaceful place. I love it. **My favourite photograph** is *Pele's Feet* by Annie Leibovitz. Great concept; great photo. She has this amazing ability to be totally trusted by the people she is photographing. They allow her to show facets of their personalities, often in an unusual format. **I believe** in life after death. It wasn't until the last 10 years that I wanted to explore my spiritual side – maybe it was an age thing. After looking at many different faiths, the person of Christ fascinated me.

Malcolm Jobling is Graphics Course Leader at Dunstable College

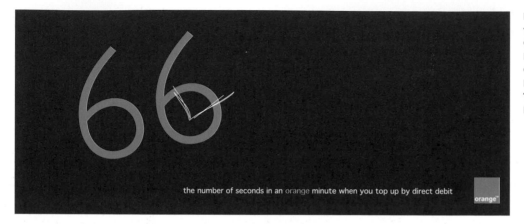

Elspeth Humphrey
ycn Username ellie
College University College, Northampton
Course BA (Hons) Graphic Design
Tutors Paul Wilson and Barry Wenden

Stacy Cleater
Commended
ycn Username 94699400
College Ravensbourne College of Design and Communication
Course BA (Hons) Graphic Design
Tutors Sian Cook and Martin Schooley
Award £600 pool allocation and creative placement at Mother

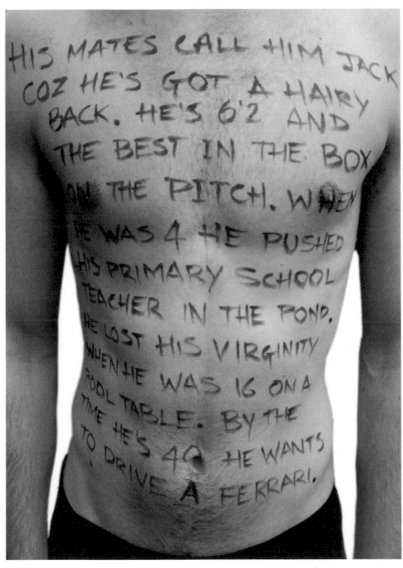

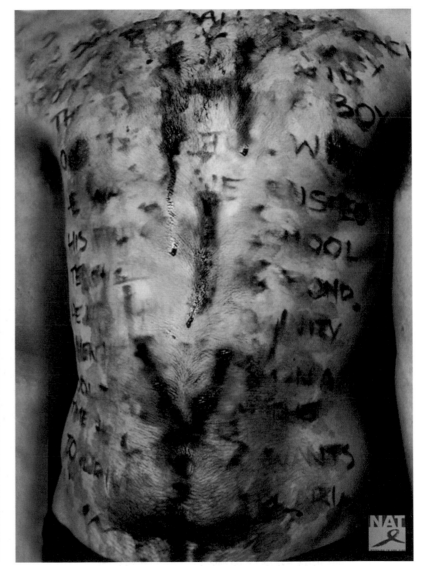

Ben Kennedy
Commended
ycn Username benkennedy
College Nottingham
Trent University
Course BA (Hons)
Graphic Design
Tutor Peter Lester
Award £750 pool allocation and

creative placement at
Saatchi & Saatchi

"Love the idea of using the
body as the medium. The lack
of fonts and the absence of a
'traditional' layout makes this
raw, direct and relevant."
Sam Jacob, Fat.

Taking the plunge is a hard thing to do – particularly when you can't tell if the pool's filled with warm water or broken glass. Leaving college is certainly a difficult step; but sometimes, staying on to take an MA can be an even braver one.

"People develop at different rates over the length of a three year course," says Caroline Roberts, editor of *Grafik* magazine. "Some people leave college ready to launch themselves into the world of work, whereas others might feel that they've only just started getting somewhere at the end of the course. The only possible reason to do an MA is because you need to develop your work and your critical skills further – there's no point in doing it just to put some extra letters after your name or because you think you'll get a bigger salary. An MA is quite different to a BA, it's more focussed on independent study and requires much more motivation."

feature

still on
COUR

"An MA is quite different to a BA, It requires much more motivation."

"We don't give students several weeks to come up with a logo. We work at a pace that reflects the industry."

One that may require more motivation than most is the MA in Creative Imaging at Huddersfield University. What makes it stand out, however, is that it was the brainchild not of academics but rather of a highly successful international advertising and design agency, Attik.

"It's not a 'fun' course," says the man behind the idea, Attik co-founder James Somerville. "I told the students to get rid of any perception of it being a normal creative postgrad."

Instead, students are worked hard on live jobs, dealing with real-life budget limitations and deadlines. It they have to work through the night alongside their professional counterparts to work on a real pitch, so be it.

"We're a commercial studio," says Somerville. "Spending time with us is a big part of the course, to understand the real pressure that you'll get. We don't give students several weeks to come up with a logo – we work at a pace that reflects the advertising industry."

The course was set up with the commercial world very much in mind. According to Somerville, it takes around six months for a new designer, fresh out of college, to become productive, which leads to smaller design studios not taking the risk of employing new graduates.

"We felt there was a large gap between those leaving design schools or colleges and working commercial designers," he says. "What we're doing is a small drop in the ocean but the idea is to help bridge that gap. There's some fantastic talent out there but they lack commercial skills."

"There were 15 of us on the course, with a variety of backgrounds." says Jonathan Hewitt, one of the course's first students when it began in October 2003 (and whose work can be seen on page 71). "The designers at Attik got very involved with what we were doing. It was quite hard work, but I think my designs are more realistic now. I feel much more commercially aware."

The benefits work two ways, of course. For Attik, it's like running a 12-month recruitment trial with a series of hand-picked students.

"Some of the students responded to the challenge of the course really well," says Somerville, "though a couple were a bit shocked by it all I think. And now we're talking to some of them about working for us. We've discovered talent that we wouldn't have found before.

"What we're also hoping is that our style of course could be replicated across the country, where a commercial design group links up with a university," he adds.

For many people, an MA course complements and extends what they've achieved at undergraduate level. As *Grafik*'s Caroline Roberts says, "You just need to find a course that suits your individual needs .

A definitive and detailed directory of all of the UK's leading postgraduate creative courses can be found in the Creative Direction section at www.ycnonline.com

we wont hand it to
you on a plate

but we will lay the table.

A career as a recruitment consultant with Michael Page International can
create a world of possibilities for the right candidate.

Michael Page
INTERNATIONAL

For further information please visit www.michaelpage.co.uk or call 02078312000

Dee McKinlay
ycn Username Dee.Mckinlay
College Edinburgh's Telford
College
Course HND Graphic and
Digital Design
Tutor Helena Goode

brand icon

top

button to heat product

bottom

chrome effect plastic

flavour strip

product directions

strong brand logo

front

back

Philip Levy
Commended
ycn Username Philip Levy
College University of
Gloucestershire
Course BA (Hons)
Graphic Design
Tutors Mike Abbey and
Vicky Baker
Award £400 pool allocation
and creative placement at JKR

"A very creative and original idea, spot on for the target market. An excellent thought process and a beautiful execution." Nick Kilby, Head of Marketing, Tetley

Keely Jackman
YCN Username keely
College Norwich School of Art
and Design
Course BA (Hons) Graphic
Design
Tutor Ray Gregory

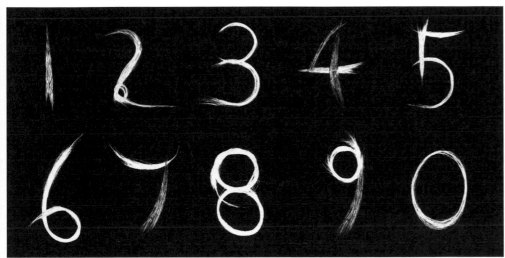

Anna-Lisa Drew
ycn Username annalisa
College Glasgow School of Art
Course BA (Hons) Visual
Communication
Tutors Susan Roan and
Sophie Morrish

Rosie Holtom
ycn Username rosieposie
College Ravensbourne College
of Design and Communication
Course BA (Hons)
Moving Image Design
Tutors Penny Hilton and
Liz Friedman

Steven Ramsay

I have no patience for caravans. Man invented shelter. Man invented the wheel. Then man puts shelter on wheels and paints shelter a non-discrete white. They are ugly, and most importantly, they are a waste of valuable metal. **My favourite car** is the Land Rover. It's British, it's proud and it's the only vehicle that looks good completely coated in mud. **I buy** *The Sun* daily, just because it costs 30p and occupies the morning train ride. **I wish someone** would invent a way of stopping annoying ring tones. Nobody wants to hear the soundtrack to *Big Brother* translated into a monotone buzzing.

Steven Ramsay is Creative Director of Cheek Design

Jonathan Hewitt and Joanne Green
Commended
ycn Username jonathew
College University of Huddersfield
Course MA Creative Imaging
Tutor Margot Short
Award £250 pool allocation

"Well-thought-through editorial design, from concept to execution, including well-written cover lines and strong punchy graphics appropriate to its audience. Energetic and unapologetic, it could do anything it wanted and do it loudly. Nice to see an entry which understood the need for clear navigation through layouts." Jeremy Leslie, Creative Director, JBCP

Julyan Mills
Commended
ycn Username julyanmills
College Falmouth
College of Arts
Course BA (Hons) Graphic
Design
Tutors John Unwin and
Mark Woodhams
Award £500 pool allocation

"Interesting idea of changing
the Durex logo to DrSex, and
linking this to sex tips fits nicely
with the brand's positioning.
The Round idea for packaging
(which better reflects actual
condom shape) plus a circular
leaflet show clear consistency
of thinking based on a product
truth. Using only colour as a
differentiator of the range
however may not be sufficient."
Eric Folliot, Group Brand
Manager, Durex

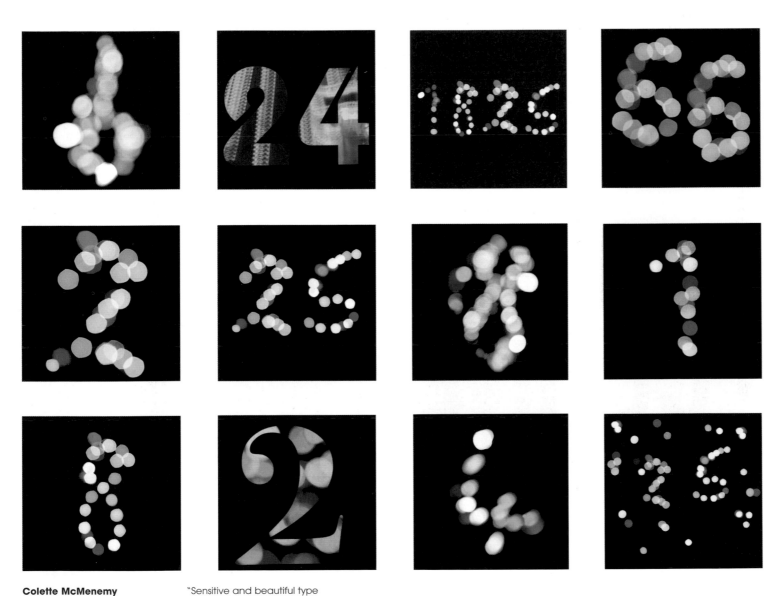

Colette McMenemy
Commended
ycn Username Colette
College Glasgow School of Art
Course BA (Hons) Visual
Communication
Tutors Steve Rigley and
Joe Petty
Award £50 pool allocation

"Sensitive and beautiful type
studies." Marie O'Connor and
Andrew Rae, Peepshow

SUPPOR
TING
YOUR
LOCAL
CORNER
SHOP

bof

Art, Music, Fashion and other Fluff

BOF MAGAZINE VOL 1 ISSUE 2

MARCH 2004

Beware of Fluff

Emily Alston
Commended
ycn username emilea
College Liverpool John Moores University
Course BA (Hons) Graphic Arts
Tutor Jonathan Hitchen
Award £250 pool allocation

"Despite a slightly unoriginal concept, this entry had strong, eclectic graphics throughout, and presented a range of layouts giving a good feel of the whole magazine."
Jeremy Leslie,
Creative Director, JBCP

Andy Rawle

There's one book on my bookshelf I've never read. I used to work at Dyson, and we were all given a copy of James Dyson's autobiography. **If I could be a fruit**, I'd be a tomato because I like to be a bit different and let people make up their own minds. **The last person** I wrote a hand-written letter to was a girl in Scotland who I met on holiday when I was 11. We met up years later and all I can say is that I wish I'd just stuck to writing letters. **My favourite cocktail** is a Harvey Wallbanger: Galliano, vodka and orange juice – a combination that led me to going home at 9.30pm from my first university ball. **I've got** some Icelandic ice fish in my fridge that was on offer. No idea what to do with it though. **I'd love** Aardman animation to make a model of me. **I have big problems** with my hair. It grows outwards like a microphone.

Andy Rawle is the Brand Manager of Brylcreem

Chris Musajjakawa
Commended
ycn Username Line-0
College Manchester
Metropolitan University
Course BA (Hons) Design
and Art Direction
Tutor Lenore Gristwood

"A clever and funny parallel
between wanting a Pot Noodle
and planning other filthy
activity!" Andy Davis, HHCL
Red Cell

Also commended
for Pot Noodle
Jennifer Doran and
Erica Latham
Stockport College
Kat Thomas
UCLAN
Their work can be seen
at www.ycnonline.com

Between the 2nd and 6th August dozens of senior figures from across the design and advertising industries were invited to the Rootstein Hopkins space at London College of Fashion to view an exhibition of commended work.

Work submitted as part of the ycn Design & Communcation Awards is initially examined by the organisations that write each brief, typically alongside the different creative agencies that they work with. They are asked to draw up a shortlist of the submissions that they feel are especially outstanding. These entries are awarded with a commendation; creative placements and financial awards are then allocated.

A selection of industry figures are then invited to view all that has been commended and are asked to identify the pieces that they feel are the most effective and original. Those who receive near-unanimous acclamation are awarded with a Rocket, which this year was designed by Nick Crosbie at Inflate for ycn. Five Rockets in total were awarded this year. **Further details about the Rootstein Hopkins space can be found at www.rhspace.co.uk**

feature
judging the ROCKET

The award winners:
Dean Pannifer (Brief: Tetley)
Neil Watts (Orange)
Petrina Bec Ying Jones
(Warburtons)
Sam McCullen (Milk
Development Council)
Tom Schofield (John Brown
Citrus Publishing)
Judges included:
James Cooper (Agency
Republic), Caroline Roberts
(Grafik Magazine), Caroline
Pay and Kim Gehrig (Mother
London), Clare Wigg (Carter
Wong Tomlin), Bruce Haines
(Leo Burnett), Jon Edge
(Interbrand), Alistair Hall
(WeMadeThis).
A full list of all those involved
in the judging can be found at
ww.ycn.online.com

**NB the above symbol
denotes that the student
has won a rocket**

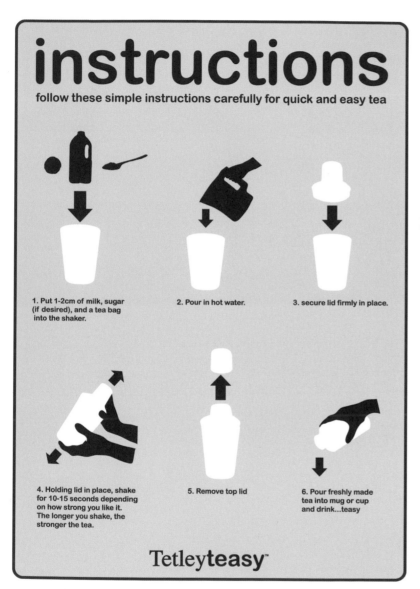

instructions

follow these simple instructions carefully for quick and easy tea

1. Put 1-2cm of milk, sugar (if desired), and a tea bag into the shaker.

2. Pour in hot water.

3. secure lid firmly in place.

4. Holding lid in place, shake for 10-15 seconds depending on how strong you like it. The longer you shake, the stronger the tea.

5. Remove top lid

6. Pour freshly made tea into mug or cup and drink...teasy

Tetleyteasy™

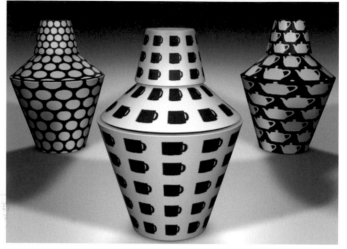

Sam Roberts
Commended
ycn Username Sam Roberts
College Hastings College
Course HND 2D-3D Design
and Communication
Tutors David Fowler
and Andrew Aloof

"A wonderfully original
approach to the brief."
James Cooper, Creative
Director, Agency Republic

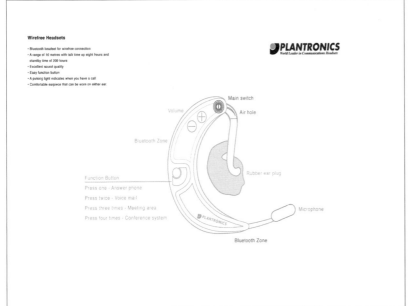

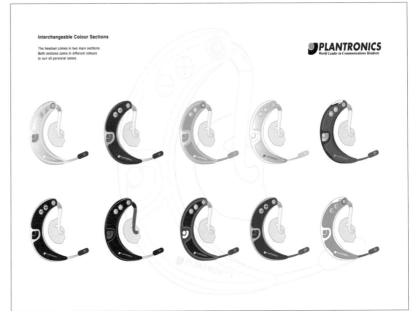

Frances Bille
Commended
ycn Username fb1981
College University of
Gloucestershire
Course BA (Hons)
Graphic Design
Tutors Mike Abbey
and Vicky Baker
Award £500 pool allocation

Also commended
for Plantronics
Carl Palmer
Kent Institute of Art and Design
Carl's work can be seen
at www.ycnonline.com

Sarah Wall
ycn Username wallo
College University of Brighton
Course BA (Hons)
Graphic Design
Tutors Lawrence Zeegen, Martin
Andersen and Siobhan Keaney

David Twardawa
ycn Username Twardawa
College University College,
Northampton
Course BA (Hons)
Graphic Communication
Tutors Paul Wilson
and Barry Wenden

Dean Pannifer

My favourite plants are daisies. Simple, iconic, versatile – you can't really go wrong with a nice daisy. **I would love** to be really good at the guitar. Music has always been very influential for me, but I've never had the patience to be good at creating it. **The best journey of my life** was the first time I went from home to Glasgow. Not the train journey itself, but moving to a new city with such a different culture was hugely inspiring. **If anyone were to play me in a film**, it would have to be a young De Niro. I love gangster films. It would also be good to hear him perfect the Geordie accent. **On my desk** there's a big pile of felt tips that don't work, crayons, pencils, inks, paints, old brushes, lots of papers, sketchbooks, flyers, magazines, photos, CDs, postcards, tea cups and a laptop hidden somewhere underneath it all. **I would love to work** with the Tango brand or with The Designers Republic – I've been a fan for as long as I can remember.

Dean's work is on page 26

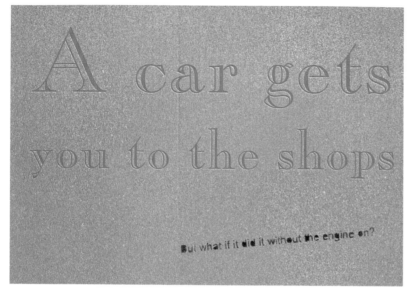

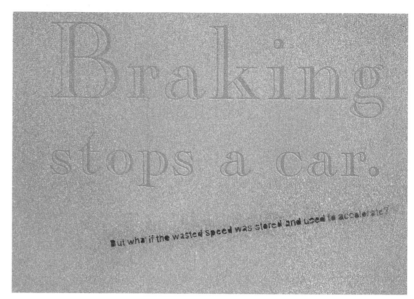

**Rick Dodds and
Stephen Howell
Commended
College** Buckinghamshire
Chilterns University College
Course BA (Hons) Graphic
Design and Advertising
Tutor Zelda Malan
Award £1500 pool allocation
and creative placement
at Saatchi & Saatchi

"This work was highly original
and the overall idea stood out
above the rest of the
submissions. Looking at the
rationale that they put together
with the creative, 'driving has
inhibitions' does not seem to be
the real insight (there are not
really inhibitions of driving).
However, we feel the creative
idea being communicated is
more 'what if' and the new
order of motoring supported by
the revolution of hybrid
technology. The mechanic of
stating established motoring
perceptions (set in stone), and
then challenging those with the
Lexus Hybrid position marked on
in graffiti, was strong. The graffiti
suggests a sense of rebellion
and revolution around hybrid
technology. The work entered
felt like more of a teaser
campaign and it would have
been good to see how the
creative idea could have been
developed. However, overall the
work was highly original
and communicated both the
benefits of Lexus Hybrid and
the sense of disruption the
technology will create in
the motoring market."
Louise Everett, Lexus GB

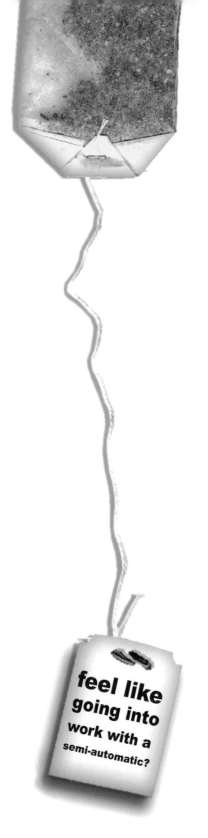
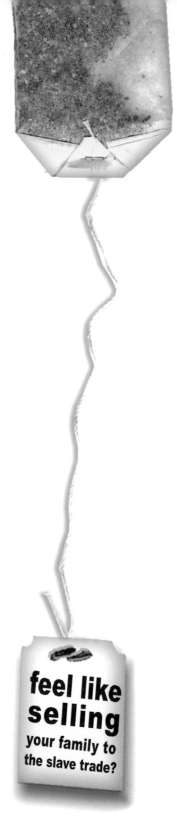
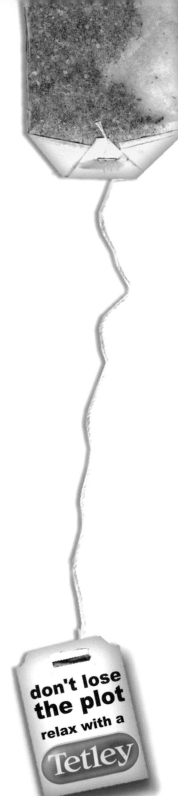

feel like
going into
work with a
semi-automatic?

feel like
selling
your family to
the slave trade?

don't lose
the plot
relax with a
Tetley

**Claire Punter
Commended
ycn Username** RUCLP

"A great execution of a
lovely idea." Nick Kilby,
Head of Marketing, Tetley

Donna Baitey
Commended
ycn username dbaitey
College Dunstable College
Course HND Graphic Design
Tutors Malcolm Jobling
and Nick Jeeve
Award £200 pool allocation
"The socks execution is a great
way to take the brand back to
real life." James Cooper, Agency
Republic

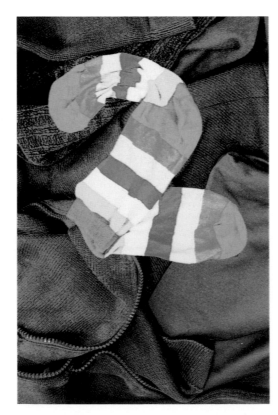

**Sarah Batten and
Tanswee Ling
Commended
ycn Usernames** marzipan pig
and reirei
College Central Saint
Martins College
Course BA (Hons)
Graphic Design
Tutor Clive Chalis
Award £600 pool allocation
and creative placement
at TBWA\GGT

"Most on-brief work
we saw, encouraging
'talkability'. Good tone of voice.
Leverages the product benefits
more than any other campaign
and showcases the different
parts of the product relevant to
students. The campaign
seemed to give the brand a
real freshness which is a sign of
some really good work. Very
well-presented ideas and a
clear and concise rationale that
did a great job of selling the
work. The use of media and
sound art direction saw that
students were spoken to in the
right place in the right tone. The
only negative we could come
up with was a lack of the 'We
Love It' strapline." Rosie Harrison,
The Sun

Zelda Malan

I hate being an Aries. It's a dodgy sign and when you admit to it, people look at you in a funny way. I've never read anything about Arians that wasn't damning and too close for comfort.
I worry about the price of Sherbet Fountains these days. **My favourite piece of furniture** is either an old display case from a shop, which I keep some of my first-issue Action Man comics in, or my new widescreen telly. **I always** choose the aisle seat, it's closer to the bloke with the tea trolley. **It's taken me two years** to remember my own phone number. **Ten years ago** I was in the unhappy state of not having been lucky enough to land the jammy jobs I find myself in now. In 10 years' time, I hope I'm not queueing up for the afternoon bingo, next to OAPs and my unemployed ex-students. **Writing lists** helps me remember things, when I remember to read them. **The best view in the world** is at the Odeon Leicester Square, Row C, seat 46.

Zelda Malan is a tutor at
Central St Martins College

Dan Collins
Commended
ycn Username Dan Collins
College Nottingham
Trent University
Course BA (Hons)
Graphic Design
Tutor Peter Lester

Justin Gridley
ycn Username justin gridley
College Bath Spa
University College
Course BA (Hons)
Graphic Design
Tutors David Beaugeard,
Paul Minott and Jack Gardner

Daniel Fernandes
ycn Username danfernandes
College University of the
West of England
Course BA (Hons)
Graphic Design
Tutors Rob Kettel and
John Hammersley

Adele Ryder
Commended
ycn Username adele
College University of Derby
Course BA (Hons)
Graphic Design
Tutor Leo Broadly

Also commended for
National Aids Trust
Gurnham Singh Thander
University of Derby
Gurnham's work can be
seen at www.ycnonline.com

Senan Lee
Commended
ycn Username SenanL
College Central Saint
Martins College
Course BA (Hons) Graphic
Design – Advertising
Tutor Alan Baines

"Great media placement.
The brand has presence in the
arena of grubby expressions."
Andy Davis, HHCL Red Cell

Frauke Stegmann

My favourite part of the body is the brain, because within its soft, whitish mass of nervous substance it possesses a magical capacity to turn the objective neuronal activity of the eye into the subjective, interpretative, intuitive self-conscious 'I', which gives us the capacity to experience awe and beauty. **Hungover**, I have been to a cafe on Hackney Road for a sober vegetarian fry-up. I have also been to the British Museum. **The films I have seen most** are *The Idiots*, *Festen* and Kurasawa's film in which Toshirô Mifune stars. **My last holiday** was to Africa on my own, to visit my ancestors. **The most useful invention ever** is pizza, because it is a tomato's consequence and I love tomatoes. **I do not carry** anything in my pockets, therefore I carry up to two bags at a time: one is a fabric print by Abake made into a bag for me by Kajsa of Abake, and the other one is Alex Rich's SHOP LOCAL bag. **I use** a soft, dark pen that can endure extreme handling. **What makes me cringe** are copycats that can't get it right – but I really love tomcats, huge hairy ones.

Frauke Stegmann is a professional illustrator.

Tom worries about the wellbeing of his HIV positive friend...

she never looks before crossing the road.

www.knowHIVworries.com
0800 567 123
NAT

Jessica worries about her HIV positive friend using her lipstick...

She thinks she looks better in it than her.

www.knowHIVworries.com
0800 567 123
NAT

Steve worries about what his friend might have brought him back from Africa...

last time he brought him back a tacky souvenir.

www.knowHIVworries.com
0800 567 123
NAT

Charlotte Johns
Commended
ycn Username cjohns
College Ravensbourne College of Design and Communication
Course BA (Hons) Graphic Design
Tutors Sian Cook and Martin Schooley
Award £750 pool allocation and creative placement at Saatchi & Saatchi

"A great strategy and strapline but felt that work was needed on the art direction." James Cooper, Creative Director, Agency Republic

abcOne
is a magazine by nobody in particular
about nothing in particular. it is an
examination of everyday life. a
proclaimation that it is ok to be
normal. it aims to encourage a
generation constantly bombarded
with globalisation and mass celebrity
to believe that what everyday people
say and do is interesting, important,
enlightening and real. contact:abcOne_magazine@hotmail.com

Will Hodgson
Commended
ycn Username BillyBoy

"Refreshingly honest, a
magazine about nobody for
nobody. Strong type on covers,
typography on reverse slightly
disappointing. A strong concept
piece that doesn't quite stand
up as a real magazine,
being too slight." Jeremy Leslie,
Creative Director, JBCP

feature

read the SMALL

Always read the small print, Grandma used to say. The problem was, the small print was so boring. Investments may go down as well as up. Not real size. Statutory rights are not affected. Serving suggestion. Shake well before opening. Batteries not included. Mixed at air studios by David Andrew for Seethink Productions. Gee, Grandma, do I have to read any more?

But recently, the small print has started to become the most interesting part of certain brands. Take innocent smoothies. On the side of their fresh juices, there's a warning: "Separation may sometimes occur (but Mummy still loves Daddy)." Or take Kit Kat. Wrappers now carry a cute cartoon of an anthropomorphic K depositing litter into that criss-crossed litter bin so beloved of 1970s Keep Britain Tidy campaigns. The message reads 'Have a tidy break'. Or take Hellmann's. The barcode is now shaped like a jar of mayonnaise. Lilt cans sport a relaxed hammock lounger depositing can in bin. Package designers, it seems, are finally having some fun.

In a sense, this is part of a fundamental shift in the role of design. In the old days, the message was simple – give us a logo/cover that stands out on the shelf and make it something we can own. It gave us all those legendary brand identities: Coca-Cola, Heinz Beans, *Rolling Stone*, the Sex Pistols and *Star Wars*. It gave us names and typefaces that simply couldn't be

Things change. Babies grow up into big fat hairy men, acorns become oak trees and once we saw a magician change a frog into a rabbit. We thought it was about time we changed a bit, so we're going to put our smoothies into big 1 litre cartons as well as bottles. The great thing is that they keep our drinks fresher for longer, and contain exactly the same recipes as ever. We hope that you enjoy them, and if you have any thoughts about us growing up, email haventyougrown@innocentdrinks.co.uk

YOUR RECOMMENDED | ALWAYS 100%

Keep refrigerated 0-5C
before and after opening.
Once opened, consume
within 2 days.
For use-by date see cap.
Gently pasteurised, like milk.
Shake it up baby.
250ml℮

innocent ©
pure fruit smoothie

mangoes & passion fruits

used anywhere else, so iconic was their status. But, at the end of the day, it was basically the design equivalent of the company yelling at the consumer in huge letters 'BUY OUR NEAT STUFF!' No real problem there, but this philosophy began in the explosion of creativity that marked out Madison Avenue in the 1950s and 1960s and it stayed in place for 30 years. It had become boring and irrelevant to the consumer.

"I think you find that, at the end of the 1990s with recession looming, there was pressure on ad budgets at the same time that clients realised advertising couldn't do the whole job," explains Stephen Bell, creative director at Coley Porter Bell, who recently revamped Cadbury's Buttons with a series of jokes on the back for kids to collect. "Advertising can lead you to temptation, but the pack is the temptation. At the same time you have a cultural difference between America and Europe. Americans like being sold to, while Europeans like to buy. As a result, designers over here probably have a little more power in the decision-making process than our American counterparts – and you've seen us leading the way in this area, while America is still very much logo, weight and barcode."

It's not always a solid design education that leads to this new wave of European thinking. When innocent launched in April 1999, it was the idea of three university chums, Richard Reed, Adam Balon and John Wright. They approached another college mate, Dan Germain, who was working as an English teacher, and persuaded him to come on board to help out with some writing they needed doing. He was charged with putting together the drinks labels, and was trying to think of something clever when the company hit another snag.

"It became clear that we didn't have enough money for a marketing budget," Germain explains. "And we were launching into a market where the likes of Coca-Cola and Proctor and Gamble were operating. We looked at our labels and saw this space usually filled with things like 'statutory rights not affected'. We thought, 'when people buy our drinks, we've got five minutes when our product is in their hands. Let's make that our time to have a conversation with them.' For one thing, it would save cash on focus groups."

Since then, innocent's labels have become a sort of newsletter/research tool. Questions about recipes or products fill the labels. The company's London festival, Fruitstock, is plugged every August. If a member of staff has a baby, the labels let the drinkers know. If the company is hiring, the first place for the ad is the labels. And at the bottom of every label is the message 'If you're bored, call us on the banana phone and we'll try to cheer you up.'

"We probably write two to three hundred different labels a year," Germain says. "On the upside, that means that if a label is bad, it's not around for long. They do get responses. We have a People's Champion in the office, Rowena, who works full time on answering people's requests and queries. She deals with between one and 300 contacts a week. Some people do complain – we've had people unhappy about 'Mummy still

loves Daddy', for instance – but it probably works out nine in favour to one against."

Design Bridge were approached by consumer pharmaceuticals giant Roche with a brief on a toothpaste brand they'd had on the shelves for years and done nothing much with. Called Punch & Judy, it was hardly shaking things up in a sector where even the best work rarely wins D&AD prizes. Taking the social responsibility of kids toothcare seriously, Design Bridge weaved cartoon characters, health messages and fun design tweaks into the package design.

"We went back to the Victorian idea of Punch and Judy," Design Bridge's CEO Jill Marshall explains. "The box became a Punch and Judy theatre with a window resembling a seaside proscenium arch cut into the side. You could see the Punch and Judy characters biffing each other with toothbrushes on the actual tube inside. Above the window we had a little message, 'Showtimes twice daily at 8am and 6pm', to help mum convey the cleaning times."

On the back of the box, Mr Punch's arch-nemesis, the crocodile, jousts with a long orange toothbrush, the bristles of which are the barcode. Atop the black spindles sits a swirl of branded toothpaste, making the statutory obligation to carry the barcode into a pun that works for both kids and parents.

It's not just fast moving consumer goods brands that are playing in this area. Mark Farrow at Farrow Design has been shaking up CD design, putting track listings on the spine to allow more space for visuals. Over in skatewear, clothing brand Howie's has been working with Carter Wong Tomlin on a series of projects that began with a t-shirt bag design, moved in-store with some customised wardrobes (above right), extended to the website and found its apogee in Howie's latest product – base layer clothing, an expensive technical range that acts a wick to conduct sweat away from the body and thus control temperature.

"There's a lot of technical information about base layer clothing that we had to get on to the box," explains Neil Hedger at the agency. "We took traditional weather symbols and used them graphically to explain how the clothing functions in a very visually-lead, simple-to-understand way. The images are so strong and the information so well presented that people spend way more time looking at the back of the box than the front. The time will come when the back of the pack is the most important branding space."

Hedger says it's the mark of a good designer. Can you take the duff stuff and make it sing? "I teach at Norwich Art College and there's a second year student there who's created a pack for own-brand nuts – cashews, peanuts and so forth – and made the 'Warning: May Contain Nuts' label the most prominent part of front of pack. It's almost a branding message. In food, that's really important. Consumers are deeply wary of the small print, so if you take it and make a feature of it, they trust you more. You're saying that you've got nothing to hide."

This is a good point. All of the innovations discussed so far are coming from a design-lead space, but food packaging design in particular is about to enter a far stickier world – the

world of government regulation. Right now the only obligation designers have with the small print on food is weight, barcode, ingredients, company contact information and best-by date. With obesity a front-page issue, however, food labelling is coming under ever closer scrutiny.

In the summer, breakfast cereal giant Kellogg's decided to redesign all their packs to show the sugar, salt, fat and calorie content on new easy-to-understand labels. The company will also let parents know how much exercise the kids need to burn off the calories in a portion. In part, this is a response to a recent Consumers Association report criticising even All-Bran for containing four times as much salt as a bag of roasted peanuts. In part, it's a bid to head off legal restrictions by showing companies can self-regulate. As this book went to press, Kellogg's were still humming and hawing about how the design job was going to work, so regretfully declined to run through their thinking with us. "We are looking at how we market our products responsibly and how we engage with consumers," was all their PR chief Chris Wermann would say.

For Jill Marshall at Design Bridge, however, this is just the start. "We ran a series of focus groups last year looking at the threat of obesity and food labelling, and we found a great deal of suspicion among consumers," she said. "There's a feeling that companies are hiding the truth about their products, and people aren't happy. This is an area where back of the pack can help – it can be the front line of any company that is prepared to demonstrate true social responsibility."

For some designers, acting as conduits for complex social messages is going to be a nightmare. For others, it's not just a challenge, it's a way of rising to the name 'designer'. "It's the small details of a product or a brand that generate the best ideas," Hedger argues. "In a sense, a design brief is all small print and it's up to us to prove our worth by making it work."

"Will back-of-pack sell more product? Will back-of-pack become more important than front-of-pack? Realistically – no," concludes Coley Porter Bell's Stephen Bell. "I would be naïve to think that every consumer will spot these subtleties on every occasion. But for those that do, the sense of discovery is highly rewarding. This is an invitation to interact with the brand, to buy into its promise that many will find hard to resist. And from a creative perspective, it's opened up a whole new area of expression."

Stephen Armstrong is a contributing editor at Wallpaper*

Simon Leahy
Commended
ycn Username simonleahy
College Stockport College
Course BA (Hons) Advertising
Tutor Mel Levic

**David Goss,
Daniel Morris and
Andrew Zeiderman
Commended
ycn Username** Gossy53
College Central Saint
Martins College
Course BA (Hons) Graphic
Design – Advertising
Tutors Clive Challis, Zelda Malan
and Maggie Souter
Award £1500 pool allocation
and creative placement at
Poulter Partners

"Some interesting ambient
ideas here along with some
excellent ones for press, poster
and DM. It would be interesting
to see how this could have
been developed for the shop
channel. It must also be said
that the critical element of
informing consumers how to bet
was missed here." Mark Saxby,
Poulter Partners

Deborah Lyal
Commended
ycn Username debz
College Glasgow School of Art
Course BA (Hons)
Visual Communication
Tutors Steve Rigley
and Joe Petty
Award £250 pool allocation

"A strong concept reflecting websites such as ebay and the whole re-use culture. The use of colour and pictures in confident, bold page layouts perfectly reflected this concept. We particularly liked the ET layout." Jeremy Leslie, Creative Director, JBCP

Marie Ronn and Stine Hole
Commended
College Central Saint
Martins College
Course BA (Hons) Graphic
Design – Advertising
Tutor Zelda Malan

Hannah Eliasson
Commended
ycn Username Birmingham
College Birmingham Institute
of Art and Design at UCE
Course BA (Hons)
Visual Communication
Tutor John Lowe

"Very strong images that would certainly get the attention and make people think differently about tea. Unsure how well this goes about communicating the new range of teas available but a wonderfully striking piece of work." Nick Kilby, Head of Marketing, Tetley

Gail Lingard
ycn Username gaillingard
College Glasgow School of Art
Course BA (Hons)
Visual Communication
Tutors Steve Rigley and Jo Petty

Chris Humphris

If I wasn't into design, I would be Hugh Hefner. He has the best job in the world. **If I could invent a new crisp flavour**, it would have to be English breakfast, so you could enjoy the stodge without the grease. **I don't really go anywhere to think**, I just tend to switch off sometimes when I need to. Usually someone will nudge me and I'll snap out of it. **The best thing about Britain** is my one-year-old nephew, James. **The one thing I hate about technology** is the fact that all my personal details are available to anyone and I have no control over it. **My morning ritual** goes as follows: wake up, realise it's the morning and then get up at a more reasonable hour. **The last thing that shocked me** was the price of a packet of cigarettes in London.

Chris' work is on page 124

Nathalie Turton and
Danielle Emery
Commended
ycn Username nathalie turton
College Central Saint
Martins College
Course BA (Hons)
Graphic Design
Tutors Clive Challis, Zelda
Malan and Maggie Souter
Award £500 pool allocation

"A great insight into clever ways
that guys can get away with
things. It is also bold in that it
takes a barrier to drinking Ice
and turns it on its head. Also
works on the fact that the
Smirnoff Ice consumer has the
intelligence to switch between
being a ladies man, a friend, a
blokes man... this is the modern
day 'bloke'. The strategy is
based on a brilliant insight but
we felt that the execution could
be evolved to become a bit
more original and smart.
Something to think about would
be how this can this be done in
an original way whilst allowing
the character to retain his
credibility." Nicola Miller, Assistant
Brand Manager, Smirnoff Ice

Also commended
for Smirnoff Ice
Helen Lumby and
Charlotte Smalley
Buckinghamshire Chilterns
University College
Jahmin Pama and
Mariannna Iacovou
University of Middlesex
Their work can be seen
at www.ycnonline.com

Michael Lawson
Commended
ycn Username michaellawson
College Dunstable College
Course BA (Hons) Graphic
Design and Business
Management
Tutors Malcolm Jobling
and Nick Jeeves

"A strong concept and a good
strapline although we were
worried that this creative could
be a bit disturbing!" Andy
Rawle, Brand Manager,
Brylcreem

Also commended
for Brylcreem
Claire Booton and
Kelly-Ann Davies
UCLAN
Their work can be seen
at www.ycnonline.com

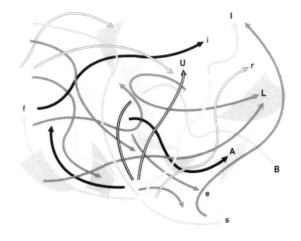

feature

creative
DIRE

contacts

CREATIVE DIRECTION

ycn Creative Direction is a brand new recruitment initiative in a dedicated section of the ycn website. It's aimed at young design and advertising creatives – those still studying or who have recently graduated, as well as those with industry experience.

The aim of Creative Direction is to continually connect young creatives with industry recruiters by centrally presenting opportunities in the form of jobs, placements and postgraduate courses online. These opportunities are supported by specially commissioned editorial content, to help people make more informed applications.

Visit **www.ycnonline.com/creativedirection** for full details and to see all of the latest job, placement and course opportunities.

The visual identity for ycn Creative Direction was designed by Monica Pirovano at the The Chase, London. Presented on the following pages is artwork demonstrating the identity and other ideas that arose along the way. The supporting comments are from The Chase, London's creative director Harriet Devoy.

The Reality Check advertising idea

Once the cheesy cap and gown photos have been installed on mantle-pieces across the country, there is the grim reality of the thousands of new design graduates having to get out there and get themselves a job.

We see 'Creative Direction' acting almost as a reality check for recent graduates, an initiative to tell them the truth, to present them with opportunities and to inform them how to go about applying for them (and perhaps more importantly, how not to go about applying for them).

We came up with the idea of graduation photographs covered with captions saying things like "Being nice is not enough". We liked the idea of a harsh tone but with enough humour to keep it interesting. We thought it would be funny to get all of the senior figures from the industry who contribute to the site to supply their graduation photos.

The literal 'direction' route

We felt that an arrow route was appropriate. After all, the initiative is all about sending people in the right direction. We thought something quite unexpected, perhaps a weathervane, would be an interesting twist on the arrow idea.

CTION

jobs   placements   post-grad   editorial
                                   courses

Final designs for Creative Direction by The Chase, London

general

Alex Braxton and Amy Gould
Commended
ycn Usernames AlexBraxton
AmyGould
Award £750 pool allocation
and possible placement at
HHCL Red Cell

"Brilliantly takes the idea of filth
and illicit temptation in store.
Very funny, on brand and who
wouldn't be able to resist
having a look. Very brave and
confident to cover your brand
up at point of purchase."
Andy Davis, HHCL Red Cell

VO: Because students take more interest in traffic control than anyone else, we think it's fair to offer them cheaper car insurance.

Graeme Bowman
Commended
ycn Username zuton_fever
Course BA (Hons) Advertising
College University of
Central Lancashire
Tutors Lin Sinclair and
Mike Moran
Award £750 pool allocation
and creative placement

at MWO

"Clever use of typical student behaviour to make the point. Simple, relevant and fabulous."
John O'Sullivan, Chairman, Mortimer Whittaker O'Sullivan Advertising

Also commended
for Direct Line
Daniel Holden
University of the West of
England
Chris Musajjikawa
Manchester Metropolitan
University
Lewis Gregory
Stockport College
Their work can be seen
at www.ycnonline.com

Stella Tsoupeli
Commended
ycn Username Stellix
College London College of
Music and Media
Course BA (Hons) Advertising
Tutors Steve Middleditch
and Vernon Churcher

"Clever surprising placement
makes this a brilliantly simple
ambient idea." Andy Davis,
HHCL Red Cell

David Spoor
Commended
ycn Username brahma_bean
College Blackburn College
Course BA (Hons)
Graphic Design
Tutor Helen Mathers

"Made us laugh! Good thinking
which ties in very well with
laddish culture. Billboard could
be executed with live bird seed.
A good campaign."
Andy Rawle, Brand Manager,
Brylcreem

The modern apple. Have you ever asked yourself how many chemical products are required to bring this perfect, almost tasteless, fruit to your table? Guess at least once before you read on. From fertilizers to pesticides to preservatives, the number can total more than 30. The health and environmental dangers are obvious, but there is something more profound in the apple as well. It's a simple question: who decided, Who chose the road, for all of us, that turned a sun and water snack into a chemical process?

post magazine

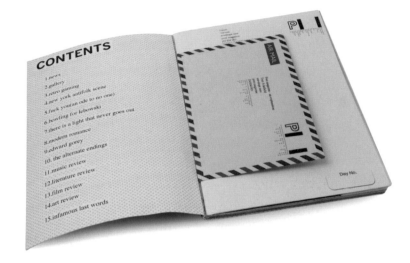

~

Tom Schofield
Commended
ycn Username TSCH
College University of
Glamorgan
Course BA (Hons) Graphic
Communications
Tutor Gerald Emanuel
Award Rocket and
£500 pool allocation

"A really great concept that challenges the traditional format and layout of magazines. The concept, content and design hold together to form a magazine that feels precious to hold and exciting to open up. Loads of interesting bits of ephemera and content throughout – each person would read it in a different way; an experience. Putting aside the production issues involved in manufacturing this, we can imagine this working for real." Jeremy Leslie, Creative Director, JBCP

SHOWCASE

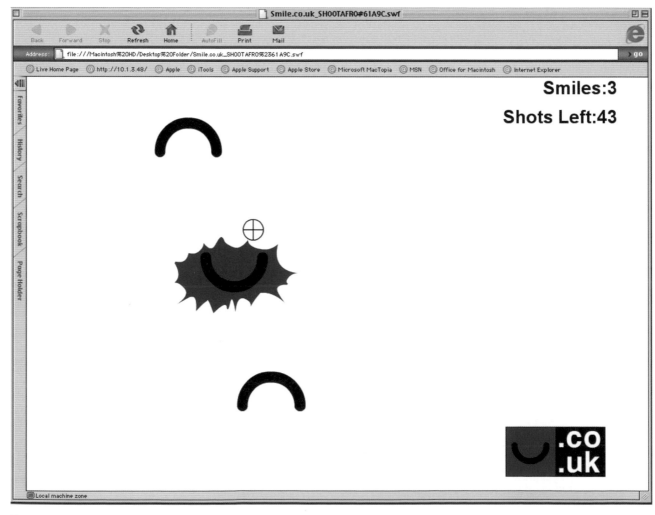

Russell Isabelle
ycn Username ru55el
College University of the
West of England

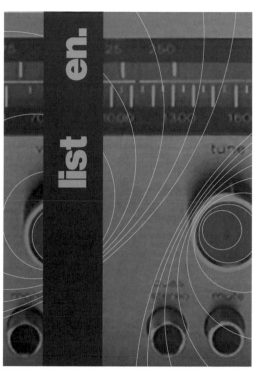

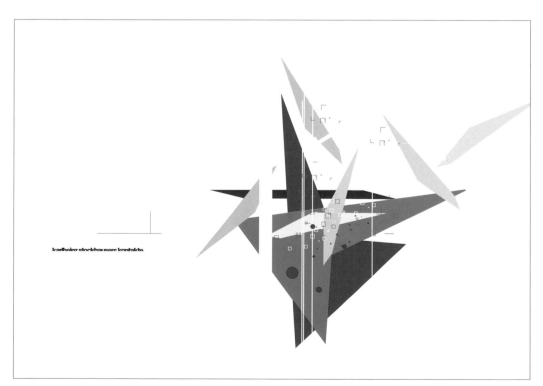

Richard Bowater
Commended
ycn Username rbowater
College Liverpool John Moores
University
Course BA (Hons) Graphic Arts
Tutor John Young

"Brave concept for the age
group – a classical music
magazine, well presented and
thought through. The design was
clean and well worked but
lacked warmth, a problem
perhaps when trying to interest
an audience in something they
might not immediately think was
for them." Jeremy Leslie,
Creative Director, JBCP

Sarah Batten and Tanswee Ling
Commended
ycn Usernames marzipan pig and reirei
College Central Saint Martins College
Course BA (Hons) Graphic Design
Tutor Clive Challis
Award £250 pool allocation

"The deep fill campaign is a great way of dramatising the deep fill range. An excellent and varied use of varied POS media that perhaps required a little more thought to consistency in look and feel."
Larry File, Marketing Manager, Ginsters

Al Young

I like to think I'd be brave enough to fight in the Second World War. It was a race war and, like a typical liberal, I can tolerate anything apart from intolerance. **The best TV presenters** for me are the parodies of TV presenters. Chris Morris does this very well. **There's only one song** I can, with any real confidence, sing all the words of: *Tequila* by The Champs (1958). **The best thing about being in charge** is that it's possible to gear an operation to reflect the way I like to do things.

My favourite piece of technology is the motion picture camera. It's the best story-telling device ever invented. **I don't tend** to get professionally jealous. I'm regularly humbled and inspired by others people's ideas. I only really get jealous of blokes over 30 with full heads of lovely hair. **My favourite advertisement** is Graham Cappy and Alan Moseley's first ad for Drum Cider. I love it because it is sexually perverse and entirely innocent at the same time. It made me laugh so much I nearly suffocated. **If the universe is infinite**, there's an alien somewhere saying the same things right now.

Al Young is Creative Director at St Luke's

Chris Humphris
Commended
ycn Username cdhumphris
College Falmouth College
of Arts
Course BA (Hons) Graphic
Design
Tutors John Unwin and
Mark Woodhams

"Demonstration of idea
progression and thought
process was excellent, as well as
the presentation of the overall
project which was among the
best of all the entries. The
interview, which shows the
thorough approach, and the
search for consumer insight
were most interesting indeed. I
think the designs are very
strong, with each sub brand
having a single colour for clear
differentiation. The font chosen is
excellent and works well with
the futurist element of the
packaging. I am not sure there
is enough information on the
front of pack to prompt a
purchase decision as the name
of a condom does not
necessarily say enough about
the product. I like the link with
the Durex X of the holder
shape. The condom container is
excellent, but the question I
have is with regard to the
multipacks of condoms – ie:
larger than a 3 pack. I thought
that adding the name to the foil
was also good for people who
take condoms out individually
(eg: in a wallet)." Eric Folliot,
Group Brand Manager, Durex

BRYLCREEM HAS CHANGED ITS LOOK...

...WHY DON'T YOU?

Kristy Powell
Commended
ycn Username powellkristy
College UCLAN ·
Course BA (Hons)
Graphic Design
Tutors Jayne Souyave, Andy
Bainbridge and Pete Thompson
Award £250 pool allocation

"A bold attempt to modernise
the brand and to create a
premium brand.
Very strong postcard/
outdoor idea using
a clear and simple execution."
Andy Rawle, Brand Manager,
Brylcreem

Mark Slack
Commended
ycn Username Slacky
College Loughborough
University School of Art
and Design
Course BA (Hons) Visual
Communication (Illustration)
Tutor Andrew Selby

"Using the language of
condoms varieties makes eating
Pot Noodle extra filthy. Very
funny." Andy Davis,
HHCL Red Cell

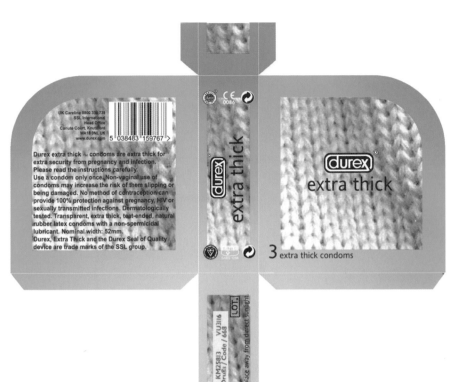

Emily Hallsworth
Commended
ycn Username moomin
College Hull School of Art and
Design
Course BA (Hons) Graphic
Design
Tutors Julie Husband
£500 pool allocation

"Excellent packaging design construction that is feasible in terms of manufacturing but also practical and visually appealing. The on-shelf impact and differentiation with the competition is also crucial. The design work is simple and visuals are well chosen for the samples provided. I think the size and types of fonts may need improving on some packs where these are unable to compete with the design in the background. I am also unclear about the framing device of the colour around the pack – would the images chosen gain from bleeding around the edges of the pack for greater impact? Overall, excellent work and I would have liked to see a point-of-sale unit which was closer to the packaging design." Eric Folliot, Group Brand Manager, Durex

Emily Alston

My favourite shape is a square with curved corners. I don't know if it has a name. **If I could make laws**, I'd ban people from eating smelly food on trains, create a compulsory dancing day and make something free for everyone... perhaps fruit and veg for a healthier nation. **I don't have a favourite trivia subject**, but if I did it definitely wouldn't be musicals. **The greatest thinker of our time** is my friend Neil. I'm sure we will all witness his genius soon. **In the last dream I can remember**, I received a text message from McFly asking me to do some work for them. **My heroes** are my dad and whoever invented stabilisers and inflatable armbands. I wouldn't have got past the age of six without them. **In my bag** I keep enough rubbish to fill a big bin, keys (sometimes), phone, minidisk player, wallet (with no money), a little notebook to write stuff in and make me look intelligent and interesting when alone in cafés, and for some bizarre reason, a spoon.

Emily's work is on page 74

I REFUSE TO CLEAN ON A Sun**DAY**

I DON'T 'DO' WORK ON A Sun**DAY**

Andrew Sheldrick
Commended
ycn Username sheldrick
College Birmingham Institute of
Art and Design at UCE
Course BA (Hons) Visual
Communication
Tutor John Lowe
Award £150 pool allocation

"Very well-presented concepts, good range of media and synopsis of each bit of work. The 'Every day is a Sunday' campaign would certainly strike a chord with students, which is half the battle won. The use of items like the 'do not disturb's and eye masks are fine examples of good ideas being carried through to final execution. The pop-ups were really on brand and the calendar looked cool. The thought behind the beer mats was also bang on and the text copy was original."
Rosie Harrison, The Sun

Also commended for The Sun
Caroline Lisowicz
Caroline's work can be
seen at www.ycnonline.com

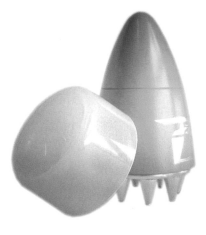

I aim for Brylcreem to compete against brands such as L'oreal and Toni & Guy. Shifting current product placement from Grecian hair dye to Wella. My research involved reviewing present popular culture, and 1950's to '60s art and design. I gathered images of products, past technology and 1950's culture. I found inspiration through aeroplane motors/engines, Cadillac, '50's interiors, a laundrette, mopeds, the Bat Mobile and a cat brush. I wanted to create a 1950's interpretation of hairstyling for the future.

My design incorporates applying wax and sculpting hair both at the same time. The application is simple. The wax stick can screw up and down at a twist, with the shaping teeth acting as a grade, allowing the user to adjust how much wax they wish to apply. The rubber teeth also shape and groom the hair, whilst massaging the head creating a textured effect. The user then may twist back the stick and replace the lid.

Jack Bannerman
Commended
ycn Username jackbann
College Sheffield Hallam University
Course BA (Hons) Packaging Design
Tutors Claire Lockwood and Glynn Hawley

"An interesting and really innovative concept that pushes the brand forward."
Andy Rawle, Brand Manager, Brylcreem

Milk has lots of calcium

cows can be milked two or three times a day!

Tracey O'Toole
Commended
ycn Username tot
College Birmingham Institute of
Art and Design at UCE
Course BA (Hons) Visual
Communication
Tutor John Lowe
Award £100 pool allocation

"Excellent packaging and
wonderful use of grass and
cows. Loved the balloons too."
Philippa Stagg, Milk
Development Council

Also commended for
Milk Development Council
Sarah Williams
Loughborough University
School of Art and Design
Eileen Renaudon
Newcastle Under
Lyme College
Their work can be seen
at www.ycnonline.com

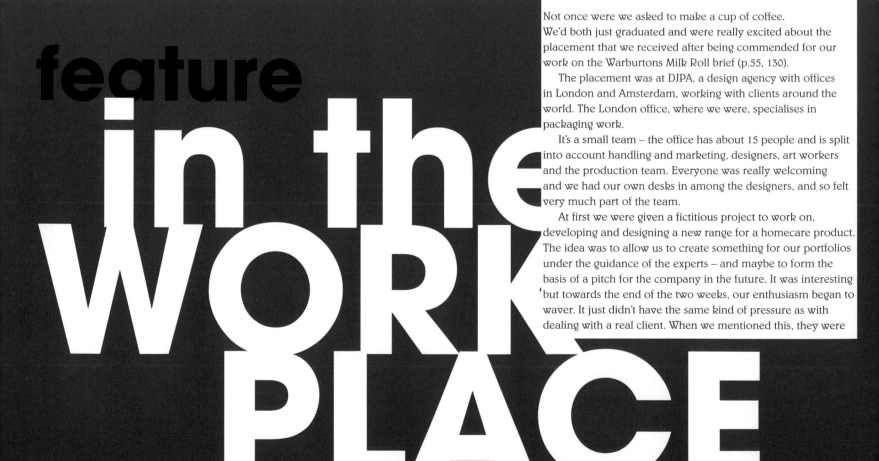

feature

in the
WORK
PLACE

Not once were we asked to make a cup of coffee. We'd both just graduated and were really excited about the placement that we received after being commended for our work on the Warburtons Milk Roll brief (p.55, 130).

The placement was at DJPA, a design agency with offices in London and Amsterdam, working with clients around the world. The London office, where we were, specialises in packaging work.

It's a small team – the office has about 15 people and is split into account handling and marketing, designers, art workers and the production team. Everyone was really welcoming and we had our own desks in among the designers, and so felt very much part of the team.

At first we were given a fictitious project to work on, developing and designing a new range for a homecare product. The idea was to allow us to create something for our portfolios under the guidance of the experts – and maybe to form the basis of a pitch for the company in the future. It was interesting but towards the end of the two weeks, our enthusiasm began to waver. It just didn't have the same kind of pressure as with dealing with a real client. When we mentioned this, they were

sympathetic (though why should they give two students an important job?) and, to our surprise, towards the end of the second week we were given a more active part in helping with a live brief for a large food company.

We'd both done placements before but this was by far the most relaxed office we'd been into. DJPA was a great place to get used to the idea of office life and real clients. Now we're just waiting for the opportunity to kick start our careers as superstar designers…

Petrina Bec Ying Jones and Cheryl Scowen were commended in the ycn Design & Communication Awards 03/04

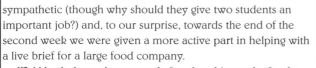

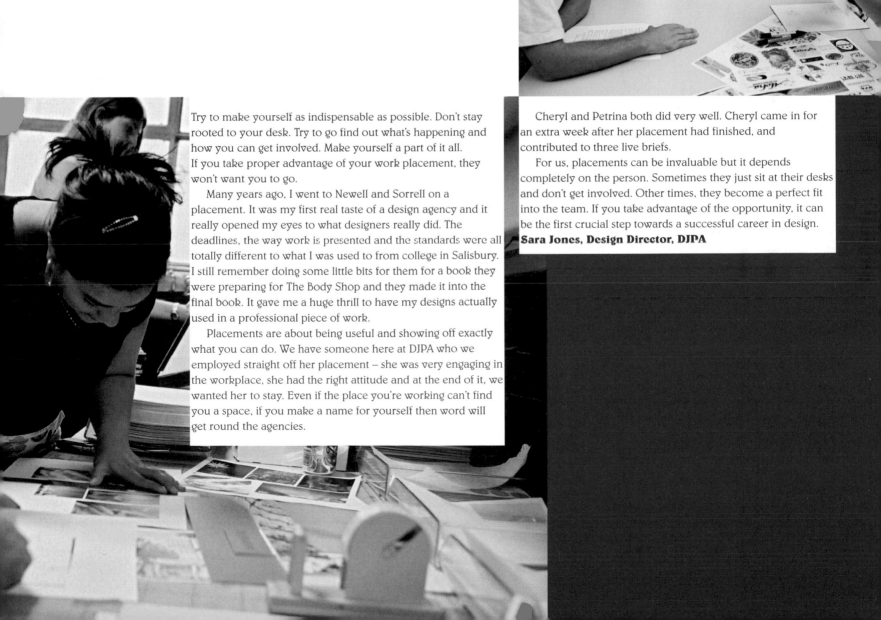

Try to make yourself as indispensable as possible. Don't stay rooted to your desk. Try to go find out what's happening and how you can get involved. Make yourself a part of it all. If you take proper advantage of your work placement, they won't want you to go.

Many years ago, I went to Newell and Sorrell on a placement. It was my first real taste of a design agency and it really opened my eyes to what designers really did. The deadlines, the way work is presented and the standards were all totally different to what I was used to from college in Salisbury. I still remember doing some little bits for them for a book they were preparing for The Body Shop and they made it into the final book. It gave me a huge thrill to have my designs actually used in a professional piece of work.

Placements are about being useful and showing off exactly what you can do. We have someone here at DJPA who we employed straight off her placement – she was very engaging in the workplace, she had the right attitude and at the end of it, we wanted her to stay. Even if the place you're working can't find you a space, if you make a name for yourself then word will get round the agencies.

Cheryl and Petrina both did very well. Cheryl came in for an extra week after her placement had finished, and contributed to three live briefs.

For us, placements can be invaluable but it depends completely on the person. Sometimes they just sit at their desks and don't get involved. Other times, they become a perfect fit into the team. If you take advantage of the opportunity, it can be the first crucial step towards a successful career in design.
Sara Jones, Design Director, DJPA

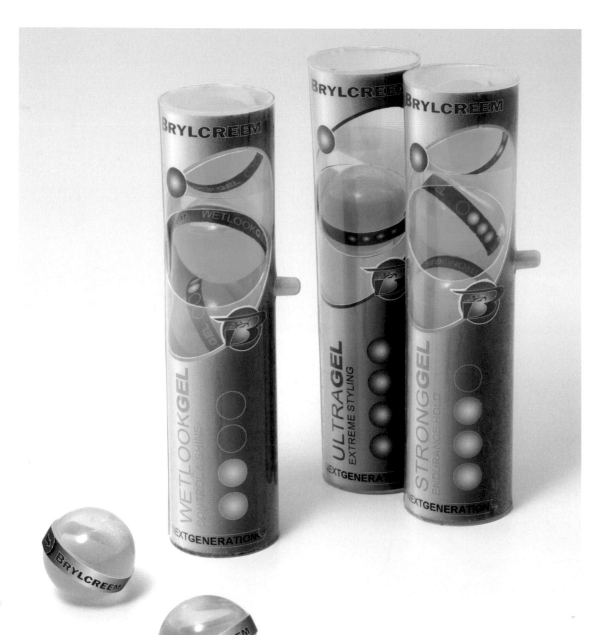

Rikki Payne
Commended
ycn Username trickyrikki
College Surrey Institute of Art
and Design University College
Course BA (Hons)
Packaging Design
Tutors Catherine Slade-Brooking
and Jack Blake
Award £750 pool allocation

"An excellently researched
and thoroughly thought-out
project of the highest quality.
Wonderfully presented and
highly original." Andy Rawle,
Brand Manager, Brylcreem

Rachel Wigley
Commended
ycn Username wigleyrd
College University of Glamorgan
Course BA (Hons) Design for Media
Tutor Gareth Hughes

"Packaging design for single condoms like 'Babybel' is a great idea and I think the tear strip is a nice idea to facilitate access. Texture and design reflecting the sub-brand benefits is simple and international. Such a design also appeals to all consumers. I also like the tube of condoms and would be interested to see how it could work where there is no texture or flavour differentiator, for example where thickness or lubricant levels are different." Eric Folliot, Group Brand Manager, Durex

Also commended for Durex
Andrew Lloyd
University College Northampton
Vanessa Kazmierski
University of Salford
Their work can be seen
at www.ycnonline.com

Tom Crabtree

I would love to play the part of Navin R Johnson in the film *The Jerk*. **If I could talk to me when I was 18**, I'd say: 'Don't get a tattoo yet. Wait a few years until your visual tastes have matured.' **If I had a racehorse**, I would let my wife name it. **The best decade for imagination** was the 1970s. Everything had a crude air of ad hoc experimentation about it. People weren't afraid of getting things wrong or looking stupid. **The most memorable character** from my childhood is my brother. **I find footwear** I like quite difficult to find. For the moment, I just settle for the old Converse 'Chuck Taylor'. Although I did have a pair of Marc Jacobs once that I loved, but I can't seem to find them anymore. **Today I have** on me £5.33. Usually, I have £10 or under. I'm forever needing a cashpoint. It's psychological I think. If I know it's in the bank and not in my wallet, I feel a bit happier. **Spelling** is an important part of being a good communicator. How can someone take what you're saying seriously if you cannot communicate it correctly?

Tom Crabtree is a graphic designer at MadeThought

Branding the bag

After some colour experimentation with the bag I have decided to keep the colour scheme simple. Too many colours and patterns distracted the attention away from the label too much. I have chosen a beige bag with a white top. Both of these colours feature in the brand palette and represent cream, milk and calcium – all elements of the Warburtons product.

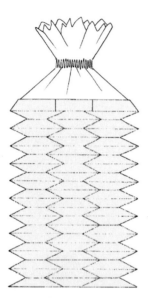

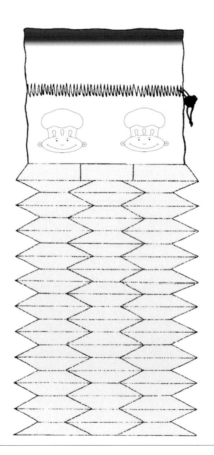

So that when the label is removed the bag is still clearly branded by Warburtons Milk Roll. I have decided to tip the top of the white plastic with the logo colours in a gradated fashion so as they are recognisable yet subtle and add an element of stand-out on the shelf without being overpowering.
I have also put the baker boy face on the white plastic so as to make the bag fun for children while still linking the bag to the brand.

Cheryl Scowen
Commended
ycn Username Chez534
Course Surrey Institute of Art and Design University College
Course BA (Hons) Packaging Design
Tutors Catherine Slade-Brooking and Jack Blake
Award £500 pool allocation

"We were impressed by the depth of preparation and strategic thought evident in this submission."
Lesley Wallwork, Marketing Manager, Warburtons

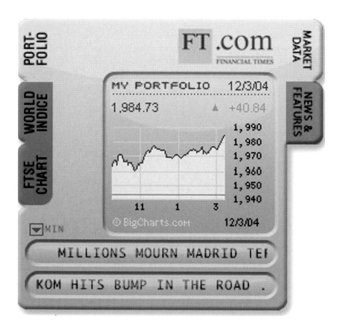

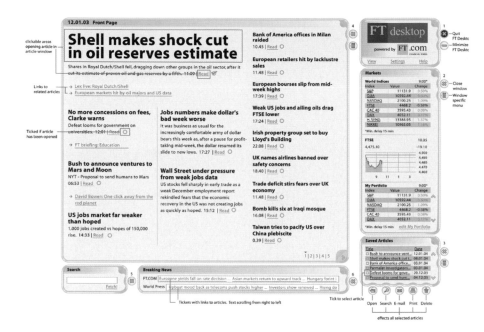

John Stuart
Commended
ycn Username yoshimi
College Edinburgh Telford
College
Course HND Graphic and
Digital Design
Tutor Helena Good

"An excellent and compact
design that provides instant
access to all key FT.com areas
without feeling too intrusive
within a desktop environment.
The ticker design is very clever
and we liked the natural way
that stories were presented with
a simple link through to FT.com."
Mat Braddy, Product Marketing
Manager, Financial Times

Carl Eriksson
ycn Username carlpaul
College UWIC
Course BA (Hons) Graphic
Communication
Tutors Olwen Moseley, Ruth
Dineen and Wendy Keay Bright

"Clever use of multiple
windows, excellent icon design
and overall really on brand
and reflective of the main
FT.com site."
Mat Braddy, Product Marketing
Manager, Financial Times

**Joanne Blaker and
Laura Bullock
ycn Username**
mightoftenmoths
College Buckinghamshire
Chilterns University College
Course BA (Hons) Graphic
Design and Advertising
Tutors Dan Williams, John
Hazlewood and Bruce Ingman

Luke Williamson

I've always loved the cut of Cooper Black, but probably because of my exposure to it through the *Peanuts* books as a kid. It just seems unique and eternally positive. **The last photograph I took** was of a statue of Yoda at the Skywalker Ranch in San Francisco. Honestly. **If I could take two things to a desert island**, I'd take my girlfriend and my son. **Music** always helps me work. Sometimes you need it to block out noise, other times you need stuff to get you going or help you concentrate. All sorts of music really, from noisy guitars to something very quiet. I tend to stick to the more traditional instruments, nothing too avant garde, thank you. **There's nothing on the wall of my bedroom** apart from cobwebs. **If I could live anywhere**, I'd go somewhere with good surf and peace and quiet. South-east Brasil, maybe. **What is the meaning of life?** Who cares.

Luke Williamson is group creative director and art director at Mother

SURPRISE ME.

phone
fax
mail
visit

20/20
20-23 Mandela Street,
London, NW1 0DU
020 7583 7071
WWW.20.20.CO.UK
Tracy Cheung

999 Design Group
91/93 Great Eastern Street,
Shoreditch, London, EC2A 3HZ
020 7739 3945
www.999design.co.uk
Aileen Geraghty

AD Creative Consultants
The Royal Victoria,
Patriotic Building, Trinity Road,
London SW18 3SX
020 8870 8743
www.adcreative.co.uk
John Graham

Allen International
Berghem Mews, Blythe Road,
London W14 0HN
020 7371 2447
www.allen-international.com
Gary Harris

Astound
1st Floor, Jessica House,
London SW18 4LS
020 8871 9066
www.astoundingfish.net
Nick Chapman

Avvio Design
Highfield Farm,Crazies Hill,
Wargrave, Berkshire RG10 8PU
01189 404444
www.avvio.co.uk
Duncan Gardener

Bite
11 Northburgh Street,
London EC1V 0AH
020 7253 2500
www.anotherbiteidea.com
Elin Tivemark

Bloom Design
25 The Village, 101 Arnies St.
London SW11 2JW
020 7924 4533
www.bloom-design.com
Gavin Blake

Blue Marlin
Circus Mews House, Circus Mews,
Bath BA1 2PW
01225 310444
www.bluemarlinbd.com
Antonia Ecklsley

Bostock and Pollitt
9-10 Floral Street,
London WC2E 9HW
020 7379 6709
www.bostockandpollitt.com
Nick Pollitt

Boxer
14 James St. Covent Garden,
London WC2E 8BU
01675 467050
www.boxer.uk.com
Paul Cattledind

Brahm Design
The Brahm Building,
Alma Road, Headingley,
Leeds LS6 2AH
01132 304000
www.brahm.com
Paul Nichols

Brandhouse WTS
10a Frederick Close,
London W2 2HD
020 7262 1707
www.brandhousewts.com
Emma Staveacre

Brewer Riddiford
69 Shelton St, Covent Gdn,
London WC2H 9HE
020 7240 9351
www.brewer-riddiford.co.uk
John Wynne and Clare O'Brian and
Steve Booth

Browns
29 Queen Elizabeth Street,
London SE1 2LP
020 7407 9074
www.browns-design.co.uk
Chris Wilson

C Eye
James House, 22-24 Corsham Street,
London N1 6DR
020 7490 2393
www.c-eye.co.uk
Michael Sheridan

Carter Design Group
North Lane, Foxton,
Leicestershire LE16 7RF
01858 433322
www.carterdesign.co.uk
Allen Stewart

Carter Wong Tomlin
29 Brook Mews, London W2 3BW
020 7569 0000
www.carterwongtomlin.com
Phil Carter

Checkland Kindleysides
Charnwood Edge, Cossington,
Leicester LE7 4UZ
01162 644700
www.checkind.com
Judith Randall

Cimex Inc
64 Essex Road, Islington,
London N1 8LR
020 7359 4664
www.cimex.com
Az Mohammed

Coley Porter Bell
18 Grosvenor Gdns,
London SW1W 0DH
020 7824 7700
www.cpb.co.uk
Deborah Leak

Communiqué 360
52 Worple Way, Richmond,
Surrey TW10 6DF
020 8940 4444
www.communique-group.com
Tim Petherbridge

Conchango
Heritage House, Church Road,
Egham, Surrey TW20 9QD
01784 222222
www.conchango.com
Charlotte Cook

Conran & Partners
22 Shad Thames, London SE1 2YU
020 7403 8899
www.conranandpartners.com
Katy Clarke

Conran Design Group
90-98 Goswell Road,
London EC1V 7DF
020 7566 4566
www.conrandesigngroup.com
Liz Jeavans

Corporate Edge
149 Hammersmith Road,
London W14 0QL
020 7855 5888
www.corporateedge.com
Ruth Aspalla

Coutts Retail Communications
Violet Road, London E3 3QL
020 7510 9292
www.crc-uk.com
Carol Judge

Creative Leap
Northburgh House,
10 Northburgh St, London EC1V 0AT
020 7549 0700
www.creativeleap.com
Richard Haywood

Crescent Lodge
Foundation House, Perseverance
Works, London E2 8DD
020 7613 0613
www.crescentlodge.co.uk
David Lovlock

Dalziel and Pow
5-8 Hardwick Street,
London EC1R 4RG
020 7837 7117
www.dalziel-pow.co.uk
Rosalyn Scott

Delaney Design Consultants
42 Prospect Rd, Tunbridge Wells,
Kent TN2 4SH
01892 523427
www.delaneydesign.co.uk
Mr or Mrs Delaney

Design Bridge
International Design Consultants,
18 Clerkenwell Close,
London EC1R 0QN
020 7814 9922
www.designbridge.com
Kirsty Rasserty

Design House
Perkin House, 1 Longlands Street,
Bradford, West Yorkshire BD1 2TP
01274 378848
www.thedesignhouse.com
Jeff Gray

Design UK
12-14 Denman Street, Piccadilly,
London W1D 7HJ
020 7292 2700
www.designuk.com
Christian Hoper

Dew Gibbons
49 Tabernacle Street,
London EC2A 4AA
020 7689 8999
www.dewgibbons.com
Nikki Campbell

Din Associates
32 St Oswald's Place,
London SE11 5JE
020 7582 0777
www.din.co.uk
Wendy Hawker

DJPA
Unit I-4, 22-24 Torrington Place,
London WC1E 7HF
020 7470 6700
www.djpa.com
Alia Naqvi

DNA Consulting
2&7 Brewery Sq., Butlers Wharf ,
London SE1 2LF
020 7357 0573
www.dna.co.uk
Jo Marvell

Dutton Merrifield
Langford Lodge, 109 Pembroke
Road, Clifton, Bristol BS8 3EX
01173 179293
www.dutton-merrifield.co.uk
Carol Gardener

DVA
7/8 Campbell Court, Bramley, Tadley,
Hampshire RG26 5EG
01256 882032
www.dva.co.uk
Barry Gibson

E3 Media
2nd Floor, The Tobacco Factory,
Raleigh Road, Southville,
Bristol BS3 1TF
01179 021333
www.e3media.co.uk
Wesley Hogg

Elmwood
Ghyll Royd, Guiseley,
Leeds LS20 9LT
01943 870229
www.elmwood.co.uk
Julia Ramsey

Emperor Design Consultants
Zetland House, 5/25 Scrutton Street,
London EC2A 4HJ
020 7729 9090
www.emperordesign.co.uk
Neil Davies

Enterprise IG
Burgoine Quay, 8 Lower Teddington
Road, Hampton Wick,
Surrey KT1 4ER
020 8943 9555
www.ksdp.com
Jo Saker

Enterprise IG
11-33 St John Street,
London EC1M 4PJ
020 7559 7000
www.enterpriseig.com
Justin Reed

Felton Communication
2 Bleeding Heart Yard,
London EC1N 8SJ
020 7405 0900
www.felton.co.uk
Kate Felton

Finisterre
The Shiva Building, The Tanneries,
Bermondsey Street,
London SE1 3XH
020 7357 9333
www.finisterre.co.uk
Sean Lewis

FLB
De La Bere House, Bayshill Road,
Cheltenham GL50 3AW
01242 245851
www.flb.co.uk
Colin Mechan

Four IV Design Consultants
Exmouth House, 3 Pine Street,
London EC1R OJH
020 7837 8659
www.fouriv.com
Holly Budgen

FPP Design
The Court Yard, 1 Dinsdale Place,
Newcastle upon Tyne NE2 1BD
0191 261 6662
www.fppdesign.com
Carol Pettinger

Fraserdesign
The Barns, London Road, Bourne
End, Hertfordshire HP1 2RH
01442 200400
www.fraserdesign.com
Andrew Fraser

Gyro Group
603 The Chambers, Chelsea Harbour,
London SW10 0XF
020 7351 1550
www.gyrocreative.com
Darren Bolton

Haygarth
Haygarth House, 28-31 High Street ,
Wimbledon Village,
London SW19 5BY
020 8971 3300
www.haygarth.co.uk
Martin Steel

Hunter Lodge Design
171 High Street, Rickmansworth,
Hertfordshire WD3 1AY
01923 714949
www.hunterlodge.co.uk
Mike Stonelake

Imagination
25 Store Street, South Crescent,
London WC1E 7BL
020 7323 3300
www.imagination.com
Sally Crabb

Innocence
85 Strand, London WC2R 0DW
020 7554 1200
www.innocence.co.uk
Georgina Collins

Interbrand
85 Strand, London WC2R 0DW
020 7554 1000
www.interbrand.com
Andy Payne

Interesource
50-52 Paul Street, London EC2A 4LB
020 7613 8200
www.interesource.co.uk
Ian Howlett

Intro
42 St. John Street,
London EC1M 4DL
020 7324 3244
www.intro-uk.com
Jo Marsh

Jack Morton Inc
16-18 Acton Park Estate, Stanley
Gardens, The Vale, London W3 7QE
020 8735 2000
www.jackmorter.co.uk
Fiona Lawlor

Johnson Banks
Crescent Works, Crescent Lane,
Clapham, London, SW4 9RW
020 7587 6400
www.johnsonbanks.co.uk
Kath Tudball

Jones Knowles Ritchie
128 Albert Street, London NW1 7NE
020 7428 8000
www.jkr.co.uk
Lou Smith

Kugel
55 Greek St, London W1D 3DT
020 7478 8300
www.kugel.co.uk
Phil Birchall

Lambie Nairn
6-18 Acton Park Estate,
Stanley Gardens, The Vale,
London W3 7QE, England
020 7802 5800
www.lambie-nairn.com
Gary Holt

Lateral
Charlotte House, 47-49 Charlotte
Road, London EC2A 3QT
020 7613 4449
www.lateral.net
Su Sareen or Colin Douglas

Lloyd Ferguson Hawkins BIC
6a-10 Frederick Close, Stanhope
Place, London W2 2HD
020 7706 8762
www.lfh.co.uk

LMC
The Walmer Courtyard, 225-227
Walmer Rd, London W11 4EY
020 7727 7344
www.lmcdesign.co.uk
David Johnston

Mansfields
Bentails, Pipps Hill Industrial Estate,
Basildon, Essex SS14 3BX
01268 520646
www.mansfieldsdesign.co.uk
Ivor Frankland

Marketplace Design
Pulpit House, 1 The Sq., Abingdon,
Oxfordshire OX14 5SZ
01235 554499
www.marketplace-design.co.uk
Ria Dakin-Potts and Colin Goodall

Met Studio Design
5 Maidstone Building Mews,
72-76 Borough High Street,
London SE1 1GN
020 7378 7348
www.metstudio.com
Alex McCuig

Millini
81 Earwel Business Park, Chessington,
Surrey KT9 2NY
020 8974 3333
www.millini.co.uk
Sue Sutton

Minima Design
The Technology Centre, Framlingham,
Suffolk IP13 9EZ
01728 727000
www.minima.co.uk
Peter Jenkins and Tony Stockman

Natural Associates
55 Charterhouse Street,
London EC1M 6HA
020 7490 4575
www.naturalassociates.com
Linda Vaux

Navyblue Design
Third Floor Morelands, 17-21 Old
Street, London EC1V 9HL
020 7253 0316
www.navyblue.com
Clare Lundy

Nucleus
John Loftus House, Summer Road,
Thames Ditton,Surrey KT7 0RD
020 8398 9133
www.nucleus.co.uk
Suzanne Lykioard

Oakwood Design Consultants
7 Park Street, Bristol BS1 5NF
01179 836789
www.oakwood-dc.com
Tony Marwick

OTM
12 Goslett Yard,
London WC2H OEQ
020 7478 4400
www.otmbrand.com
Sharon Luckett

Parker Williams Design
1st Floor Boysey Hse, Barley Mow
Passage, London W4 4PT020 8995 6411
www.parkerwilliamsdesign.co.uk
Shireen Karim

PDD
85-87 Richford St., London W6 7HJ
020 8735 1111
www.pdd.co.uk
Melanie Homes

Pearlfisher
12 Addison Avenue, London,
W11 4QR
020 7603 8666
www.pearlfisher.com
Emma Turbutt

Pemberton & Whiteford
Ivor House, 21 Ivor Place,
Marylebone, London NW1 6EU
020 7723 8899
www.p-and-w.com
Lee Newham

Pierrot Print and Design
Birtley Courtyard, Birtley Road,
Bramley, Guildford, Surrey GU5 0LA
01483 899000
www.pierrot.uk.com
Monique Bure

Pocknell Studio
Pocknell, Readings, Blackmore End,
Braintree, Essex, CM7 4DH
01787 463206
www.pocknellstudio.com
David Pocknell

Point Blank Inc.
16 Gresse St. London W1T 1QL
020 7291 8320
www.pointblankinc.co.uk

David Uprichard
Poulter Partners,Rose Wharf,
East Street , Leeds LS9 8EE
01132 856500
www.poultergroup.com
John Dean

Purple Circle
Global Headquarters, 1 Howard
Street, Nottingham NG1 3LT
01159 550005
www.purplecircle.co.uk
Darren Fisk

Radley Yeldar
24 Charlotte Road,
London EC2A 3PB
020 7033 0700
www.ry.com

Ratcliffe Fowler Design
2 Chancery Place, Milstone Lane,
Leicester LE1 5JN
01162 420200
www.ratcliffefowlerdesign.co.uk
Mike Ratcliffe and James Fowler

Reading Room
53 Frith St, Soho, London W1D 4SN
020 7025 1800
www.readingroom.com
Margaret Manning and Simon Usher

Redhouse Lane Communications
14-15 Bedford Square,
London WC1B 3JA
020 7462 2600
www.redhouselane.co.uk
Helen Coffee

Refinery Marketing
Communications
10 Pitbrook Street,
Manchester, M12 6JX
0161 273 5511
www.refinerygroup.co.uk

Rufus Leonard
The Drill Hall, 57a Farringdon Road,
London EC1M 3JB
020 7404 4490
www.rufusleonard.com
David Pye

SAS
6 Salem Road, London W2 4BU
020 7243 3232
www.sasdesign.co.uk
Andrew Fleming or Steve Howell

Scream Design
174 Church Road, Hove BN3 2DJ
01273 728287
www.eventerdesign.com
Gilmar Wendt

Sedley Place
68 Venn Street, London SW4 0AX
020 7627 5777
www.sedley-place.co.uk
Karys Rowan

Seymour Powell
327 Lillie Road, London SW6 7NR
020 7381 6433
www.seymourpowell.com
Fiona Nash

Shelton Fleming Associates
35 Chelsea Wharf, Lots Road,
London SW10 0QJ
020 7351 2420
www.sheltonfleming.co.uk
Sabrina Cohen

Sheppard Day Associates
The Friary, 47 Francis Street,
London SW1P 1QR
020 7821 2222
www.sheppard-day.com
Emma Wynne

Siebert Head
80 Goswell Road, London EC1V 7DB
020 7689 9090
www.sieberthead.com
Tracey Barr

Small Back Room
88 Camberwell Road,
London SE5 0EG
020 7701 4227
www.smallbackroom.com
Rhoda Maw

Smith & Milton
The Hot House, 44-46 Sekford St.,
London EC1R 0HA
020 7608 4242
www.smith-milton.co.uk
John Rushton

Splashdown
Unit 2D + 2C Westpoint, 36-37
Warple Way, London W3 0RG
020 8222 6612
www.splashdown.co.uk
Craig Burrows

Springer Jacoby Design
159-173 St John Street,
London EC1V 4RS
020 7880 4700
www.sj.com
Mark Pritchard

Springetts Design Consultants
13 Salisbury Place, London W1H 1FJ
020 7486 7527
www.springetts.co.uk
Anke Peters or Clare Dallaghan

Start Creative
2 Sheraton Street, Soho,
London, W1F 8BH
020 7269 0101
www.startcreative.co.uk
Nicole Blight

Stocks Taylor Benson
The Forge,
Narborough Wood Park, Desford
Road, Enderby,
Leicestershire LE19 4XT
01162 387833
www.stbdesign.co.uk
Mark Smith and Martin Muir

Syzygy
4th Floor, Elsley House, 24-30 Great
Titchfield Street, London W1W 8BF
020 7460 4080
www.syzygy.net
Darren Seymour

Tayburn
15 Kittle Yards, Causewayside,
Edinburgh EH9 1PJ
0131 662 0662
www.tayburn.co.uk
Rachel Stretch

TGV Design & Marketing
St Agnes House, Cresswell Park,
Blackheath, London SE3 9RJ
020 8852 9448
www.tgvdesign.co.uk
Anita Phillips

The Chase (London)
22 Newman St., London W1T 1PH
020 7927 0821
www.thechase.co.uk
Colin Beckenham

The Chase (Manchester)
1 North Parade, Parsonage Gardens,
Manchester, M3 2NH
0161 832 5575
www.thechase.co.uk
Harriet Devoy

The Church Agency
6 Franklin Court, Stannard Way,
Priory Business Park,
Bedford MK44 3JZ
01234 404040
www.thechurchagency.com
Alan Herron

The Design Group
Bryles House, 32-34 Clerkenwell
Road, London EC1M 5PS
020 7608 1144
www.the-design-group.co.uk
Michael O'Connor

The Formation
59 Charlotte Road,
London EC2A 3QW
020 7739 8198
www.theformation-cc.co.uk
Valeria Correa

The Open Agency
Mill House, 8 Mill Street,
London SE1 2BA
020 7740 7000
www.openagency.com
Adrian Kilby

Think Farm
3rd Floor, 89-91 Wardour St,
London, W1F 0UB
020 7439 4399
www.thinkfarm.co.uk
Lindsey Ching

Turnbull Ripley
Monmouth House, 87-93
Westbourne Grove, London W2 4UL
020 7221 0110
www.turnbullripley.co.uk
Mark Norton

Turner Duckworth
Voysey House, Barley Mow Passage,
London, W4 4PH
020 8894 7190
www.turnerduckworth.com
Trebe Ripley

Tynan D'Arcy
Alexandra Court, St Leonards Road,
Windsor SL4 3BP
01753 833550
www.tynan-darcy.com
Christian Eager

Vibrandt
The Sandom Group, Old Brewery,
Russell Street, Windsor SL4 1HQ
01753 624 242
www.vibrandt.co.uk
Ian D'Arcy

Vitamin V
1 Sekforbe St, Clerkenwell,
London EC1R 0BE
020 7075 6080
www.vitiminv.tv
Greg Vallance

Ware Anthony Rust
Newnham Mill, Newnham Road,
Cambridge CB3 9EY
01223 566212
www.war.uk.com
Les Mear

Wolff Olins
10 Regents Wharf, All Saints Street,
London N1 9RL
020 7713 7733
www.wolff-olins.com
Richard Bland

Wren Rowe
4 Denbigh Mews,
London SW1V 2HQ
020 7828 5333
www.wrenrowe.co.uk
Lisa MacDonald

Ziggurat
8-14 Vine Hill, Clerkenwell,
London EC1R 5DX
020 7969 7777
www.zigguratbrands.com
Paul Foulkes and Clare Murphy

12snap
Level 5, New Bridge Street House,
30-34 New Bridge Street,
London EC4V 6BJ
020 7072 4172
www.12snap.com
Caroline Smith

Abacus e-media
6 Underwood Street,
London N1 7JQ
0870 549 1500
www.abacusemedia.com
Steven C...

Agency Republic
1 ... ange Place,
London SW1... 2BZ
020 7942 00...
www.agencyrepublic.com
James C...

Agency.com
85 Strand, London WC2R 0DW
020 7964 8200
www.agency.com
Kathy Pritchard

AKQA
Prince's House, 38 Jermyn Street,
London SW1Y 6DN
020 7494 9200
www.akqa.com
Yasmin Quemard

Amaze
Port of Liverpool Building,
Pier Head, Liverpool L3 1BZ
0870 240 1700
www.amaze.com
Helen Watson

Arc Interactive
Warwick Building, Kensington
Village, Avonmore Rd,
London W14 8HQ
020 7071 2692
www.arcinteractive.co.uk
Natt Watt

Arnold Interactive
14 Welbeck Street,
London, W1G 9XU
020 7908 2700
www.arnoldinteractive.com
Maxine Gregson

Aspect Group
Clerkenwell House, 67 Clerkenwell
Road, London EC1R 5BL
020 7504 6900
www.aspectgroup.co.uk
Hilary Wilkie

Atticmedia
34 Waterside, 44-48 Wharf Road,
Islington, London N1 7UX
020 7490 8789
www.atticmedia.com
Ross Baird

Beech2
Medius House, 2 Sheraton Street,
London W1F 8BH
020 7297 9497
www.beech2.com
Derek Hayes

Big Picture Interactive
... arade, ... ington Spa,
W...ickshi... CV32 4DG
0...4 22...
www.bigpictureinteractive.co.uk
...y De...ey

Brave Marketing
The ... e Bu...ing, ...amstead, 10
Van... Plac..., London S...Av
020 ... 1984...
www.brave.co...
David Booth

Carlson Digital
Carlson Court, 116 Putney Bridge
Road, London SW15 2NQ
020 8875 0875
www.carlson-europe.com
Matt Hall

Chemistry Communications
158 Hurlingham Road, Melbray
Mews, Fulham, London SW6 3NG
020 7736 5555
www.chemistrygroup.co.uk
Denise Myers

Cimex Media
64 Essex Road, Islington,
London N1 8LR
020 7359 4664
www.cimex.com
Az Mohammad

CMW Interactive
42-46 Weymouth Street,
Marylebone, London W1G 6NR
020 7224 4050
www.cmwinteractive.com
Jula Luwsey

Conchango
Heritage House, Church Road,
Egham, Surrey TW20 9QD
01784 222222
www.conchango.com
Charlotte Cook

Craik Jones Digital
120 Regent Street, London W1B 5RY
020 7734 1650
www.digital.craikjones.co.uk
Mark Buckingham or Lee Roberts

Cramm Francis Woolf
12 Burleigh Street,
London WC2E 7PX
020 7539 7780
www.cfw.co.uk
Lindsay Watson

cScape
4 Pear Tree Court, Clerkenwell,
London EC1R 0DS
020 7689 8800
www.cscape.com
Pera Mullan

Dare Digital
8-10 Great Titchfield Street,
London W1W 8BB
020 7612 3600
www.daredigital.com
Flo Heiss

Digit
54-55 Hoxton Square,
London N1 6PB
020 7684 6769
www.digitlondon.com
Daljit Singh

Digitas Europe
9-10 Alfred Place, London WC1E 7EB
020 7494 6700
www.digitas.com
Kelly Johnston

Digiterre
The Quadrangle, 49 Atalanta Street,
London SW6 6TU
020 7381 7910
www.digiterre.com

DLKW Dialogue
25 Wellington Street,
London WC2E 7DA
020 7836 3474
www.dlkwdialogue.com
Malcolm Green

DNA
2&7 Brewary Square, Butlers Wharf,
London SE1 2LF
020 7357 0573
www.dna.co.uk
Joe Marvel

Domino Systems
The Innovation Centre, Kingston
Bagpuize, Oxfordshire OX13 5AP
01865 821821
www.domino.com
Sue McIntosh

Dowcarter
48 Rawstorne Street,
London EC1V 7ND
020 7689 1200
www.dowcarter.com
Mark Griffis

DVA
7/8 Campbell Court, Bramley, Tadley,
Hampshire RG26 5EG
01256 882032
www.dva.co.uk
Barry Gibson

E3 Media
2nd Floor, The Tobacco Factory,
Raleigh Rd, Southville,
Bristol BS3 1TF
01179 021333
www.e3media.co.uk
Wesley Hogg

EHS Brann
6 Briset Street, London EC1M 5NR
020 7017 1000
www.ehsbrann.com
Lu Dixon

Equator
Sovereign House, 58 Elliot Street,
Glasgow G3 8DZ
0141 229 1800
www.eqtr.com
James Jepherson

Exponetic
5/51 Derbyshire Street, Bethnal
Green, London E2 6JQ
020 7613 1053
www.exponetic.com
James Bebbington

Fernhart New Media
77 Park Lane,
Croydon CR0 1JG
020 8253 0210
www.fernhart.com
Bryan Mann

Freestyle New Media Group
The American Barns, Banbury Rd,
Lighthorne, Warickshire CV35 0AE
01926 652832
www.fsnm.co.uk
Sarah Harris

Global Beach
522 Fulham Rd,
London SW6 5NR
020 7384 1188
www.globalbeach.com

Glue London
31-39 Redchurch Street,
London E2 7DJ
020 7739 2345
www.gluelondon.com
Sebastian Royce

Good Technology
332b Ladbroke Grove,
London W10 5AH
020 7565 0022
www.goodtechnology.com
Sezannah Saffet

Graphico New Media
Goldwell House, Old Bath Road,
Newbury, Berkshire RG14 1JH
01635 522810
www.graphico.co.uk
Alex Weller

Greenroom Digital
120-124 Curtain Road,
London EC2A 3SQ
020 7426 5147
www.greenroom-digital.com
Jon Hamm

Groovy Train
5-9 Hatton Wall, London EC1N 8HX
020 7400 7575
www.groovytrain.com
Paul Grier

Gurus
4 Park Royal Metro Centre, Britannia
Way, London NW10 7PA
020 8838 3007
www.gurus.co.uk
Nasir Ahmed

Head to Head Web
Tideway Yard, Mortlake High Street,
London SW14 8SN
020 8392 2022
www.headtohead.net
Francois Reynier

Hi-Res
8-9 Rivington Place,
London EC2A 3BA
020 7729 3090
www.hi-res.net
Florian Schmitt

IDNet
The Spirella Building, Letchworth,
Herts, SG6 4ET.
01462 476555
www.idnet.net
Andy Field

Inbox Media
Contact House, High Street,
Wanborough, Swindon SN4 0AE
01793 348880
www.inbox.co.uk
Gary Stevens

Incepta Online
3 London Wall Buildings, London
Wall, London EC2M 5SY
020 7282 2800
www.inceptaonline.com
Isobel Palmer

Intercea
1 Transcentral, Bennet Road,
Reading, Berkshire RG2 0QX
01189 169900
www.intercea.co.uk
Jan Watson

Interesource New Media
50-52 Paul Street,
London EC2A 4LB
020 7613 8200
www.interesource.com
Tim Malbon

IR Group
PO Box 4387, 6-10 Great Portland
Street, London W1A 7SP
020 7436 3140
www.ir-group.com
Hilla Neske

IS Solutions
Windmill House, 91-93 Windmill
Road, Sunbury-on-Thames,
Middlesex TW16 7EF
01932 893333
www.issolutions.co.uk
Jean Bushell

itraffic
82 Charing Cross Road,
London WC2H 0QB
020 7964 8500
www.itraffic.com
Kathy Pritchard

Javelin Group
71 Victoria Street,
London SW1H 0HW
020 7961 3200
www.javelingroup.com
Terry Jones

Joshua Interactive
Wells Point, 79 Wells Street,
London W1T 3QN
020 7453 7900
www.joshua-agency.co.uk
Mitch Levy

Kleber Design
3rd Floor, 95A Rivington Street,
London, EC2A 3AY
020 7729 2819
www.kleber.net

KMP Associates
Kingfisher Court, Yew Street,
Stockport, Cheshire SK4 2HG
08708 688900
www.kmpassociates.com
Andrew Peg, Nikk Smith and
John Keefe

Lateral
47-49 Charlotte Road,
London EC2A 3QT
020 7613 4449
www.lateral.net
Simon Crabtree

Lawton eMarketing
4 Grosvenor Square,
Southampton SO15 2BE
023 8082 8500
www.lawtonemarketing.com
Sarah Hornby

Lean Mean Fighting Machine
Primrose Hill Business Centre, 110
Gloucester Avenue,
London NW1 8JA
020 7722 4988
www.lmfm.co.uk
Dave Bedwood

Lightmaker
Century Place, Buildings 3 & 4,
Lamberts Road, Tunbridge Wells,
Kent TN2 3EH
01892 615015
www.lightmaker.com

Linney Design
Adamsway, Mansfield,
Nottinghamshire NG18 4FL
01623 450460
www.linneydesign.com John Kay

McCann-I
Bonis Hall, Bonis Hall Lane,
Prestbury, Cheshire SK10 4EF
01625 822200
www.mccann-i.com
Sarah Fryer

M-Corp
Somerley, Ringwood,
Hampshire BH24 3PL
01425 477766
www.m-corp.com
Chris Murdoch

Mitchell Conner Searson
Elme House, 133 Long Acre,
London WC2E 9DT
020 7420 7991
www.broadband.co.uk
Fiona Conner

Modem Media UK
183 Eversholt Street,
London NW1 1BU
020 7874 9400
www.modemmedia.com
David Bryant

Moonfish
2 Sheraton Street, London W1F 8BH
08700 70 4321
www.moonfish.com
Robert Pinfold

NetInfo
Berkshire House, Queen Street,
Maidenhead,
Berkshire SL6 1NF
01628 687800
www.netinfo.com
Carl Groth

Nucleus
John Loftus House, Summer Road,
Thames Ditton, Surrey KT7 0QQ
020 8398 9133
www.nucleus.co.uk
Suzanne Lykiard

Object1
6-8 Standard Place, Rivington Street,
London EC2A 3BE
020 7684 1800
www.object1.com
Brett Bircham

Ogilvy Interactive
10 Cabot Square, Canary Wharf,
London E14 4GB
020 7345 3000
www.ogilvy.com
Tracy Murray

Oyster Partners
1 Naorojl Street, London WC1X 0JD
020 7446 7500
www.oyster.com
Claire Myerson

Pilot Interactive
Devonshire Hall, Devonshire
Avenue, Street Lane,
Leeds LS8 1AW
01132 282359
www.pilotinteractive.co.uk
Chris Hemingway

Poke
Biscuit Building, 10 Redchurch
Street, London E2 7DD
020 7749 5353
www.pokelondon.com
Lizzie Underwood

PoulterNet
Rose Wharf, East Street,
Leeds LS9 8EE
01133 834200
www.poulternet.com
Carinne Pujara

Precedent Communications
109-123 Clifton Street,
London EC2A 4LD
020 7216 1300
www.precedent.co.uk

Preloaded
16-24 Underwood Street,
London N1 7JQ
020 7684 3505
www.preloaded.com
Paul Canty

Profero
Centro & Mandela Street,
London NW1 0DU
020 7387 2000
www.profero.com
Tina Brazil

Proximity London
191 Old Marylebone Road,
London NW1 5DW
020 7298 1000
www.proximitylondon.com
Hazel Malone

Publicis Dialog
82 Baker Street, London W1U 6AE
020 7935 4426
www.publicis-dialog.co.uk
Nick Spudzinski

Reading Room
53 Frith Street, Soho,
London W1D 4SN
020 7025 1800
www.readingroom.com
Jacki Porter

Realise
No.1 Poultry, London EC2R 8JR
0131 476 6000
www.realise.com
Andrew Craig

Recollective
Recollective Limited, Studio 2,
Alaska Building 600, 61 Grange
Road, London SE1 3BB
020 7064 4196
www.recollective.co.uk
Frances O'Reilly

Recreate Solutions
London House, 271-273 King Street,
Hammersmith, London W6 9LZ
020 8233 2916
www.recreatesolutions.com
Gigi Bettencourt-Gomes

Redhouse Lane
14-15 Bedford Square,
London WC1B 3JA
020 7462 2600
www.redhouselane.co.uk

Redweb
Quay House, The Quay, Poole,
Dorset BH15 1HA
08451 303010
www.redweb.co.uk

Redwood New Media
7 Saint Martin's Place,
London WC2N 4HA
020 7747 7226
www.redwood-newmedia.com

Reflex Digital
Host Media Centre, Leeds,
West Yorkshire LS7 3HZ
0113 20 7017
www.reflex.net

Rufus Leonard
The Drill Hall, 57A Farringdon Road,
London EC1M 3JB
020 7404 4490
www.rufusleonard.com
Steve Howell

Sapient
1 Bartholomew Lane,
London EC2N 2AX
020 7786 4500
www.sapient.co.uk

SBI and Company UK
Elizabeth House, 5th Floor, 39 York
Rd, London SE1 7NQ
020 7071 6300
www.sbiandcompany.com
Lucy Cavallo

Screen Pages
4 The Courtyard, Wisley,
Surrey GU23 6QL
01932 359160
www.screenpages.com
Roger Willcocks

Sequence Sequence
Media Centre, Bridge Street,
Cardiff CF10 2EE
0845 1000 400
www.sequence.co.uk
Mike Prith

Splendid
199 Picadilly, London W1J 9HA
020 7287 4442
www.howsplendid.com
Dan Morris

Swamp
103 Clarendon Road, Leeds, LS2 9DF
08451 202405
www.swampme.com
Andrew Brown

Syzygy UK
4th Floor, Elsley House, 24-30 Great
Titchfield Street, London W1W 8BF
020 7460 4080
www.syzygy.net
Sasha Francis

TBG
100 Highgate Studios, 53-79 Highgate
Road, London NW5 1TL
020 7428 6650
www.tbgltd.com
Kenneth Lillie

TechnoPhobia
The Workstation,
15 Paternoster Row,
Sheffield S1 2BX
01142 212123
www.technophobia.co.uk
Andrew Pendrick

Tequila London
82 Charing Cross Road,
London WC2H 0QB
020 7557 6100
www.tequila-uk.com
Vanessa Kelly

The Big Group
91 Princedale Road, Holland Park,
London W11 4NS
020 7229 8827
www.biginteractive.co.uk
Nick Paterson-Jones

The Hub
The Power House,
1 Linkfield Road, Isleworth,
Middlesex TW7 6QG
020 8560 9222
www.thehub.co.uk
Gail Ellison

Thoughtbubble
58/60 Fitzroy Street,
London W1T 5BU
020 7387 8890
www.thoughtbubble.com
Terrance Krjezl

TMG
36 Southwark Bridge Road,
London SE1 9EU
020 7261 1777
www.tmg.co.uk
Simon Gill

Tribal DDB
12 Bishops Bridge Road,
London W2 6AA
020 7258 4500
www.tribalddb.co.uk
Ben Clapp

Unit9
43-44 Hoxton Square,
London N1 6PB
020 7613 3330
www.unit9.com
Piero Frescabaldi

Victoria Real
Shepers Building Central,
Shepherds Bush, London W14 0EE
020 8222 4050
www.victoriareal.com

WDPA Communications
142 New Cavendish Street,
London W1W 6YF
020 7323 2480
www.wdpa.co.uk

Wheel Group
Beaumont House, Kensington
Village, Avonmore Road,
London W14 8TS
020 7348 1000
www.wheel.co.uk
Gabrielle de Wardener

Wireless Information Network
1 Cliveden Office Village, High
Wycombe, Bucks HP12 3YZ
01494 750500
www.winplc.com
Barbara Green

Write Image
271 Regent Street, London W1B 2BP
020 7959 5400
www.write-image.com
Marie Ellen Brook

XM London
121-141 Westbourne Terrace,
London W2 6JR
020 7724 7228
www.xmlondon.com
Amy Watson

Zentropy Partners UK
Lynton House, 7-12 Tavistock
Square, London WC1H 9LT
020 7554 0500
www.zentropypartners.co.uk
Matthew Greenhalgh

The names included are contacts for junior creative positions and work placements

advertising

1576 Advertising
25 Rutland Square,
Edinburgh EH1 2BW
0131 473 1576
www.1576.co.uk
Adrian Jeffery

23red
2nd Floor Elsley Court, 20-22 Great
Titchfield Street, London W1W 8BE
0870 0130023
www.23red.com
Lucy Carlson

A V Browne Advertising
46 Bedford Street,
Belfast, Northern Ireland BT2 7GH
028 9032 0663
www.avb.co.uk
Mike Fleming

A Vision (London)
The Blue Building, 7-11 Lexington
Street, London W1F 9AF
020 7287 9898
www.avisionlondon.co.uk
Lydia Barklem

Abbott Mead Vickers.BBDO
151 Marylebone Road,
London NW1 5QE
020 7616 3500
www.amvbbdo.com
Emma Clark

Aerodeon
449 Oxford Street, London W1L 2PS
020 7629 0089
www.aerodeon.com
Chris Bourke

Alcazar Limited
Old Maling Pottery, Walker Road,
Newcastle Upon Tyne NE6 1AB
0191 224 4000
www.alcazar.co.uk
Hugh Cheswright

Anderson Lambert
2 Kensworth Gate, High Street,
South Dunstable, Beds LU6 3HS
01582 754000
www.andersonlambert.com
Paul Mcnally

Anderson Spratt Group
Anderson House, 409 Holywood
Road, Belfast BT4 2GU
02890 802000
www.andersonspratt.com
Philip Milnes

Arc Marketing
Warwick Building, Kensington
Village, Avonmore Road,
London W14 8HQ
020 7751 1962
www.arcmarketing.com
Graham Mills and Jack Nolan

Archibald Ingall Stretton
Berners House, 47-48 Berners Street,
London W1T 3NF
020 7467 6100
www.aislondon.com
Anna Barker

**Ardmore Advertising &
Marketing**
Pavillions Office Park, Kinnegar
Drive, Holywood,
County Down BT18 9JQ
028 9042 5344
www.ardmore.co.uk
Larry McGarry

Artavia
Artavia House, Queen Street,
Barnstable, Devon, EX32 8HW
01271 323333
www.artavia.co.uk
Mark Berridge

Atlas Advertising
10 Welbeck Street, London W1G 9YA
020 7467 3140
www.atlasadvertising.co.uk
Sarah Nash

Barkers Scotland
234 West George Street,
Glasdgow, G2 4QY
0141 248 5030
www.barkersscotland.co.uk
Nick Lang and Norrie Leckie

Barrett Cernis
77 Long Arce, London WC2E 9LB
020 7663 3575
www.barrett.cernis.co.uk
Ray Barret

Barrett Howe Group
1 Curfew Yard, Thames Street,
Windsor, Berkshire SL4 1SN
01753 869455
www.barretthowe.com
John Gittins

**Barrington Johnson Lorains &
Partners**
Sunlight House, Quay Street,
Manchester M3 3JZ
0161 831 7141
www.bjl.co.uk
Stephen Johnson

Bartle Bogle Hegarty
60 Kingly Street, London W1B 5DS
020 7734 1677
www.bbh.co.uk
John O'Keeffe

Base 01
10-12 The Causeway, Teddington,
Middlesex TW11 0HE
020 8943 9999
www.base01.co.uk
David Thomas

BDH TBWA
St Paul's, 781 Wilmslow Road,
Didsbury Village, Manchester,
Lancashire M20 2RW
0161 908 8600
www.bdhtbwa.co.uk
Danny Brook-Taylor

Beatwax
91 Berwick Street, London W1F 0NE
020 7734 1965
www.beatwax.com
Nick Roper

Big Picture Interactive
9 Parade, Leamington Spa,
Warwickshire CV32 4DG
01926 422002
www.bigpictureinteractive.co.uk
Becky Dempsey

Blair Fowles Advertising
22 St Peters Rd,
Bournemouth BH1 2LE
01202 558111
www.blairfowles.co.uk
Colin Gibson

Bond Advertising
47 Timber Bush,
Edinburgh EH6 6QH
0131 476 8053
www.bondadvertising.com
Caroline Garrad

Boy Meets Girl S&J
Fourth Floor, 159-173 St John Street,
London EC1V 4RS
020 7012 6000
www.boymeetsgirl.sj.com
Kate Stanners

Burkitt DDB
1 East Poultry Avenue,
London EC1A 9PT
020 7320 9300
www.burkittddb.com
Olga Budimir

Byron Advertising
Byron House, Wallingford Road,
Uxbridge, Middlesex UB8 2RW
01895 252131
www.thebyrongroup.com
Matthew Allen

Campbell Doyle Dye
4 Utopia Village, Chalcot Road,
London NW1 8LH
020 7859 9800
www.cddlondon.com
Dave Dye

**Charterhouse Advertising &
Marketing**
West Point, 501 Chester Road,
Manchester, Lancashire M16 9HH
0161 848 9050
www.charterhouse-advertising.co.uk
Neil Mutch

CheethamBellJWT
Astley House, Quay Street,
Manchester, Lancashire M3 4AS
0161 832 8884
www.jwt.com
Andy Cheetham

Citigate Albert Frank
26 Finsbury Square,
London EC2A 1SH
020 7282 8000
www.citigateaf.co.uk
Paul Anderson

Citigate SMARTS
100 Ocean Drive, Edinburgh EH6 6JJ
0131 555 0425
www.smarts.co.uk
Hilary Joiner and Colin Montgomery

Clark McKay Walpole
42-46 Weymouth Street, Marylebone,
London W1G 6NR
020 7487 9750
www.cmw-uk.com
Steve Walpole

**Clear Marketing
Communications**
121 Palatine Road, Didsbury,
Manchester M20 3YA
0161 448 8008
www.clearmarketing.co.uk
Tony Price and Chris Doyle

Clemmow Hornby Inge
3rd Floor, Paramount House,
162-170 Wardour Street,
London W1F 8ZX
020 7025 9890
www.chiadvertising.com
Brian Turner and Micky Tudor

Cogent Heath Farm
Hampton Lane, Meriden,
West Midlands CV7 7LL
0121 627 5040
www.cogent.co.uk
Ann Smith

Cognition
4 Dormer Place, Leamington Spa,
Warwickshire CV32 5AE
01926 330800
www.cognitionbnt.com
Peter Hughes

Comma
12 Dorset Street, London W1U 6QS
020 7935 4554
www.comma.co.uk
Terry Bush

**Corporate Marketing and
Advertising Services**
The Granary, Southill, Cornbury
Park, Charlbury, Oxford OX7 3EW
01608 811228
www.cmas.co.uk
Andy Spilsbury

**Crammond Dickens Lerner &
Partners**
1 Earlham Street, London WC2H 9LL
020 7240 8100
www.cdl-uk.com
Barnaby Dickens

Cravens Advertising
42 Leazes Park Road, Newcastle-
upon-Tyne NE1 4PL
0191 232 6683
www.cravens.co.uk
Alan Harvey

Creative Marketing Services
CMS House, 4 Spring Bank Place,
Bradford, West Yorkshire BD8 7BX
0870 381 6222
www.cmsadvertising.co.uk
Chris Hughes

Creative Media Advertising
Overton House, West Road,
Congleton, Cheshire CW12 1JY
01260 292600
www.creativenet.co.uk
Rob Simpson

Cuba Advertising
15 Little Portland Street,
London W1W 8BW
020 7637 3786
www.cubaadvertising.co.uk
Ben Wren

DDB London
12 Bishops Bridge Road,
London W2 6AA
020 7258 3979
www.ddblondon.com
Ruth Harlow

Delaney Lund Knox Warren & Partners
25 Wellington Street,
London WC2E 7DA
020 7836 3474
www.dlkw.co.uk
Debbie Simmonds

Dewynters PLC
48 Leicester Square,
London WC2H 7QD
020 7321 0488
www.dewynters.com
Bob King

Different Advertising, Design & Marketing
10 Summerhill Terrace, Newcastle-upon-Tyne NE4 6EB
0191 261 0111
www.different-uk.com
Chris Rickaby

Doner Cardwell Hawkins
26-34 Emerald Street,
London WC1N 3QA
020 7734 0511
www.doner.co.uk
Paul Cardwell

Dowcarter
48 Rawstorne Street,
London EC1V 7ND
020 7689 1200
www.dowcarter.com
John Rahim

Duckworth Finn Grubb Waters
41 Great Pulteney Street,
London W1F 9NZ
020 7734 5888
www.dfgw.com
Helen Jordan

Edmonds Advertising
23 Mitchell Street,
Edinburgh EH6 7BD
0131 467 8333
www.edmonds.co.uk
David Cowan

EHS Brann
6 Briset Street, Clerkenwell,
London EC1M 5NR
020 7017 1000
www.ehsbrann.com
Zoe Beer

Ellison Communications
The Media Building, 5 Selsdon Way,
London E14 9GL
020 7510 5900
www.ellisoncommunications.co.uk
Glenn Portch

Emberton Dale Advertising
224 Upper Fifth Street, Central
Milton Keynes,
Buckinghamshire MK9 2HR
01908 668338
www.emberton-dale.com
John Emberton

Emery McLaven Orr
The Old Rectory, Vicarage Lane,
Highworth, Swindon SN6 7AD
01793 767300
www.emo.uk.com
PJ Lane

Euro RSCG London
15 Alfred Place, London WC1 7EB
020 7467 9200
www.partnersbddh.co.uk
Kirsty Shaw

EURO RSCG Wnek
Gosper , Cuploa House, No.15 Alfred
Place, London WC1E 7EB
020 7240 4111
www.eurorscg.co.uk
Nick Casing

Factor 3 Communications
Royal House, Parabola Road,
Cheltenham,
Gloucestershire GL50 3AH
01242 254242
www.factor3.co.uk
Adrian Crane

Fallon
67-69 Beak Street,
London W1F 9SW
020 7494 9120
www.fallon.co.uk
Karina Wilshire

Family Advertising Limited
CBC, House 24, Canning Street,
Edinburgh EH3 8EG
0131 272 2704
www.familyadvertising.co.uk
David Isaac and Kevin Bird

FCB London
55 Newman Street, London W1T 3EB
020 7947 8000
www.london.fcb.com
Rachael Sanderson

Feather Brooksbank
The Old Assembly Hall, 37
Constitution Street, Leith,
Edinburgh,
Midlothian EH6 7BG
0131 555 2554
www.featherbrooksbank.co.uk

Feel
Red Dog Yard, 78 Liverpool Road,
Angel, London N1 0QD
020 7359 9600
www.feelagency.com
Steven Chandler and Chris Arnold

Fine Company
Richmond House, Otley Road,
Guiseley, Leeds LS20 8FP
01943 870870
www.fine.co.uk
Anna Wadsworth

Fire IMC
10 Dargan Crescent, Belfast BT3 9JP
02890 774388
www.fireimc.com
Adrian Power

Flint
50 Marshall Street,
London W1F 9BQ
020 7851 7800
www.flint.uk.com
Jane Maskell

Fox Kalomaski
48 Fitzroy Street, London W1T 5BS
020 7691 8090
www.foxkalomaski.co.uk
Jane Stevens

Fox Murphy
17-19 St Georges Street,
Norwich NR3 1AB
01603 621587
www.foxmurphy.co.uk
Simon Middleton

Frame C
100 Brunswick Street,
Glasgow G1 1TF
0141 559 5840
www.framecunningham.co.uk
Mark Johnson or George Cumming

frank the agency
Camellia House, 76 Water Lane,
Wilmslow, Cheshire SK9 5BB
01625 521444
www.itsfrank.com
Carl Edwards

GCAS Advertising
Russell Court, 38-52 Lisburn Road,
Belfast, N Ireland BT9 6AA
028 9032 3418
www.gcasgroup.com
Peter Ellis

Genesis Advertising
7 Crescent Gardens,
Belfast, Northern Ireland BT7 1NS
028 9031 3344
www.genesis-advertising.co.uk
Stanley Davidson

Gillett & Bevan
5 Richmond Street,
Manchester,
Lancashire M1 3HF
0161 228 0023
www.gillett-bevan.com
Alan Bevan

Gough Allen Stanley
Kembrey House,
5 Worcester Road, Bromsgrove,
Worcestershire B61 7DL
01527 579555
www.gough.co.uk
Sue Bailey

Grey London
215-227 Great Portland Street,
London W1W 5PN
020 7636 3399
www.grey.com
Polly Varnes

GSB Associates
31 St Leonards Road, Eastbourne,
East Sussex BN21 4SE
01323 722933
www.gsba.co.uk
Melissa Young

Guy Robertson Partnership
11 Ashley Street, Glasgow G3 6DR
0141 564 6000
www.grpartnership.co.uk
Guy Robertson

Hay Smith Advertising
15 Mentone Gardens,
Edinburgh EH9 2DJ
0131 623 3200
www.haysmith.co.uk
Trevor Hay

HDM Agency
98-99 Jermyn Street,
London SW1Y 6EE
020 7321 2227
www.hdmagency.co.uk
Paul Vennard and Dave Ditzel

Healthworld Communications Group
121-141 Westbourne Terrace,
London W2 6JR
020 7262 2141
www.healthworld.co.uk
Aim'ee Watson

HHCL/Red Cell
5th Floor, Kent House,
14-17 Market Place,
London W1W 8AJ
020 7436 3333
www.ehhcl.net
Lisa Hall

Hicklin Slade & Partners
Bewlay House, 2 Swallow Place,
London W1B 2AE
0207 664 0404
www.hicklinslade.com
Romy Hutchinson

Hird Advertising
Omega Court, 376 Cemetery Road,
Sheffield S11 8FT
0114 266 5289
Stuart Hird

HPS Group
Park House, Desborough Park Road,
High Wycombe,
Buckinghamshire HP12 3DJ
01494 684300
www.hpsgroup.co.uk
Steve Kendall

Huet & Co
1st Floor, 5 Ridgefield,
Manchester M2 6EG
0161 835 3100
www.huet.co.uk
Michel Huet

Image Group Jersey
1 West Centre, Bath Street St Helier
Jersey JE3 4FB
01534 734444
www.image.gg
Glen Smith

J. Walter Thompson
1 Knightsbridge Green,
London SW1X 7NW
020 7656 7000
www.jwt.co.uk
Camilla Hulyer

Karmarama
Level 5, 16 Gresse Street,
London W1T 1QL
020 7612 1777
www.karmarama.com
Naresh Ramchandani
and Dave Buonaguidi

Kinghorn-Davies Advertising
35-39 Blandford Square,
Newcastle upon Tyne,
Tyne And Wear NE1 4HW
0191 261 8666
www.kinghorn-davies.co.uk
Terry Wilson

Langham Works
32 Gosfield Street, London W1V 6ED
020 7636 5552
www.langhamworks.co.uk
Gareth John

Leagas Delaney
1 Alfred Place, London WC1E 7EB
020 7758 1758
www.leagasdelaney.com Rob Burleigh

Leith Edinburgh
37 The Shore, Leith,
Edinburgh EH6 6QU
0131 561 8600
www.leith.co.uk
Gerry Farrell

Leith London
1-4 Vigo Street, London W1S 3HT
020 7758 1400
www.leith.co.uk
Meryl White

Leo Burnett
Warwick Building, Avonmore Road,
Kensington Village,
London W14 8HQ
020 7751 1800
www.leoburnett.com
Alex Plumley

Link ICA
Media House, Hollingworth Court,
Ashford Road. Maidstone,
Kent. ME14 5PP
01622 767 700
www.linkica.co.uk
Kay Burge

LMA
LMA House, 3rd Avenue,
Southampton,
Hampshire SO15 0LD
023 8077 2888
www.lma.co.uk
Ed Chesterton

Love Creative
72 Tib Street, Manchester M4 1LG
0161 907 3150
www.lovecreative.com
Phil Skegg

Lowe
Bowater House, 68-114
Knightsbridge, London SW1X 7LT
020 7584 5033
www.loweuk.com
Ed Morris

Lowe Broadway
10-11 Percy Street,
London W1T 1DA
020 7344 8888
www.lowebroadway.com
Jacqui Rainfray

Lyle Bailie International
31 Bruce St, Great Victoria St,
Belfast BT2 7JD
028 9033 1044
www.lylebailie.com
Julie Anne Bailie

M&C Saatchi
36 Golden Square,
London W1R 4EE
020 7543 4500
www.mcsaatchi.com
Sarah Thompson

Maher Bird Associates
81 Dean Street, London W1D 3NN
020 7309 7200
www.mba.co.uk
Linn Bolton, Graham Monk

Marr Associates
Waterside House, 46 The Shore,
Leith, Edinburgh EH6 6QU
0131 555 4040
www.marr.co.uk
Colin Marr

Marten Gibbon Associates
11 Little College Street,
London SW1P 3SH
020 7340 1900
www.mga-advertising.co.uk
Ed Pollard

Martin Tait Redheads
Buxton House Buxton Street,
Newcastle-upon-Tyne NE1 6NJ
0191 232 1926
www.mtra.co.uk
Collette Maddison

McCann Erickson
7 Herbrand Street,
London WC1N 1EX
020 7837 3737
www.mccann-erickson.co.uk
Jen Piper

McCann Erickson Birmingham
McCann House, Highlands Road,
Shirley, Solihull B90 4WE
0121 7133500
www.mccann-erickson.co.uk
Alison Richards

McCann Erickson Bristol
6 King Street, Bristol BS1 4EQ
0117 921 1764
www.mccann-erickson.co.uk
John Hayward

McCann Erickson Manchester
Bonis Hall Prestbury, Macclesfield,
Cheshire SK10 4EF
01625 822200
www.mccann-erickson.co.uk
Sarah Fryer

Mearns & Gill
7 Carden Place, Aberdeen AB10 1PP
01224 646311
www.mearns-gill.freeserve.co.uk
Allen Mearns

Miles Calcraft Briginshaw Duffy
15 Rathbone Street,
London W1T 1NB
020 7073 6900
www.mcbd.co.uk
Maxine Faulkner

Minerva
Minerva House, 1-4 North Crescent,
Chenies Street, London WC1E 7ER
020 7631 6900
www.minervalondon.com
Liza Bullock

Mortimer Whittaker O'Sullivan
The Carriage Hall, 29 Floral Street,
London WC2E 9TD
020 7379 8844
www.mwo.co.uk
Ronelle Bianched

Mother
Biscuit Building, 10 Redchurch
Street, London E2 7DD
020 7012 1999
www.motherlondon.com
Nathalie Patel

Mustoes
2-4 Bucknall Street,
London WC2H 8LA
020 7379 9999
www.mustoes.co.uk
Mick Mahoney

Navigator Blue
The Baths, 18 Ormeau Avenue,
Belfast, Northern Ireland BT2 8HS
028 9024 6722
www.navigatorblue.com
Terry Corr

Nexus/H UK
Multimedia House, Hill Street,
Tunbridge Wells, Kent TN1 2BY
01892 517777
www.nexus-h.co.uk
Jacquie Baker

NMI Group
Middlesex House, 34-42 Cleveland
Street, London W1T 4JE
020 7436 5000
www.nmigroup.com

Ogilvy & Mather
10 Cabot Square, Canary Wharf,
London E14 4QB
020 7345 3000
www.ogilvy.com
Annie Scott

Ogilvy Primary Contact
5 Theobald's Road,
London WC1X 8SH
020 7468 6900
www.primary.co.uk
Daniel Forman

OgilvyOne Worldwide
10 Cabot Square, Canary Wharf,
London E14 4QB
020 7566 7000
www.ogilvy.com
Annie Scott

Omobono
Old Farm Business Centre, Church
Road, Toft, Cambridge CB3 7RF
01223 307 000
www.omobono.co.uk
Chris Butterworth

Potter Dow
Middlesex House, 34-42 Cleveland
Street, London W1T 4JE
020 7255 0200
www.potterdow.com

Poulter Partners
Rose Wharf, East Street, Leeds,
West Yorkshire LS9 8EE
0113 285 6500
www.poultergroup.com
Corrine Pujara

Profero
Centro 3, Mandela St,
London N1 0DU
020 7387 2000
www.profero.com
Tina Brazil

Proximity London
191 Old Marylebone Road,
London NW1 5DW
020 7479 8000
www.proximitylondon.com
Kaitlin Ryan

Publicis
82 Baker Street, London W1U 6AE
020 7935 4426
www.publicis.co.uk
Ingrid Osborne-Holst

PWLC
46 The Calls, Leeds,
West Yorkshire LS2 7EY
0113 398 0120
www.pwlc.com
Pete Camponi and Rick Ward

Quiet Storm
15-16 Margaret Street,
London W1W 8RW
020 7907 1140
www.quietstorm.co.uk
Becky Clarke

**Radford Creative
Communications**
Blackfriars House, Parsonage,
Manchester M3 2JA
0161 832 8807
www.radfordnet.com
Phil Atkinson

Radioville
143 Wardour Street,
London W1F 8WA
020 7534 5959
www.radioville.co.uk
Tim Craig

**Rainey Kelly Campbell
Roalfe/Y&R**
Greater London House, Hampstead
Road, London NW1 7QP
020 7404 2700
www.uk.yr.com
Kate Pozzi

Rhythmm
Trelawny House, Surrey Street,
Bristol, Avon BS2 8PS
0117 9429786
www.rhythmm.co.uk
Kevin Young

Richmond Towers
26 Fitzroy Square, London W1P 6BT
020 7388 7421
www.richmondtowers.com
Victoria Furzer

RLA Southern
Burlington House, Old Christchurch
Road, Bournemouth Dorset BH1 2HZ
01202 297755
www.rla.co.uk

Robson Brown
Clavering House, Clavering Place,
Newcastle-Upon-Tyne NE1 3NG
0191 232 2443
www.robson-brown.co.uk
Angela Foley

Rock Kitchen Harris
The Creative Mill, 31 Lower Brown
Street, Leicester,
Leicestershire LE1 5TH
0116 233 7500
www.rkh.co.uk
Tracy Scott

Roose & Partners Advertising
102 Sydney Street, London SW3 6NJ
020 7349 6800
www.roose.co.uk
Mandy Enright

Ross Levenson Harris
60-63 Victoria Road, Surbiton,
Surrey KT6 4NQ
020 8390 4611
www.rlh.co.uk
Christine Jones

RPM3
William Blake House, 8 Marshall
Street, London W1V 2AJ
020 7434 4343
www.rpm3.co.uk
Russell Wales

Saatchi & Saatchi
80 Charlotte Street,
London W1T 4QP
020 7636 5060
www.saatchi.com
Tracy Flaherty

Sans Frontiere Marketing
73 High Street, Lewes,
East Sussex BN4 1XG
01273 487800
www.sansfrontiere.co.uk
Audrey Evans

Sass
The Haybarn, Mere Hall Park,
Warrington Road, Mere,
Cheshire WA16 0PY
01565 832 832
www.puresass.com
Graham Sass

Scholz & Friends London
80 Clerkenwell Road,
London EC1M 5RJ
020 7961 4090
www.scholzandfriends.co.uk
Steve Spence

Sellers & Rogers
Price House, 37 Stoney Street, The
Lace Market, Nottingham NG1 1LS
0115 955 1159
www.sel-rog.co.uk
David Spence

Seriously Bright
William Blake House, 8 Marshall
Street, London W1F 7EJ
020 7494 2677
www.seriouslybright.com
David Delmonte

Severn Advertising
Severn House, 30 Ombersley Street,
West Droitwich Spa,
Worcestershire WR9 8QX
01905 795999
www.severnad.co.uk
Kieran Fitzpatrick

Smee's Advertising
3-5 Duke Street, London W1M 6BA
020 7486 6644
www.smees.co.uk
Anthony Smee

Solus Strategic
28 Victoria Street, Douglas,
Isle of Man IM1 2LE
01624 666 000
www.solus-strategic.com
Chris Berry

Soul
4 New Burlington Street, Mayfair,
London W1F 2JD
020 7292 5999
www.souladvertising.com
Ruth Croutch

St Lukes
22 Dukes Road, London WC1H 9PN
020 7380 8888
www.stlukes.co.uk
Trudy Baker

Stuart Hirst
7 Eastgate, Leeds,
West Yorkshire LS2 7LY
0113 243 4646
www.stuarthirst.demon.co.uk
Mike Wappett

**Target Marketing
Communications**
Brand House, 62 Painswick Rd,
Cheltenham,
Gloucestershire GL50 2EU
01242 633100
www.targetgroup.co.uk
Sharron Rudge

TBWA\GGT
82 Dean Street, London W1D 3HA
020 7439 4282
www.tbwa-ggt.com
Amber Moltze

TBWA\London
76-80 Whitfield Street,
London W1T 4EZ
020 7573 6666
www.tbwa-london.com
Danielle Bunn

Team Saatchi
83-89 Whitfield Street,
London W1A 4XA
020 7436 6636
www.teamsaatchi.co.uk
Mike Middleton

Ten Alps MTD
Great Michael House, 14 Links Place,
Edinburgh EH6 7EZ
0131 553 9200
www.tenalpsmtd.com
Euan Carmichael

The Brahm Agency
The Brahm Building, Alma Road,
Headingley, Leeds LS6 2AH
0113 230 4000
www.brahm.com

The Bridge
The Jacobean Building , 49/53
Virginia Street, Glasgow G1 1TS
0141 552 8384
www.thebridgeuk.com
Brian Crook

The JJ Group
The Clock Barn, Little Baldon,
Oxford, Oxfordshire OX44 9PU
01865 343100
www.thejjgroup.com
Sue Ingledew

**The Levy McCallum
Advertising Agency**
203 Saint Vincent Street,
Glasgow G2 5NH
0141 248 7977
www.levymccallum.co.uk
Roy L. McCallum

The Petersen Partnership
15 Windsor Place, Cardiff, South
Glamorgan CF10 3BY
029 20 729400
www.petersenpartnership.com
Haydn Evans

The Thinking Agency
Carlton House, Pickering Street,
Leeds LS12 2QG
0113 2890000
www.clarendon-am.co.uk
James Eate

The Union Advertising Agency
Union House, 18 Inverleith Terrace,
Edinburgh EH3 5NS
0131 625 6000
www.union.co.uk
Don Smith

The Works London
2-3 Melbray Mews, 158 Hurlingham
Road, London SW6 3NS
020 8233 1600
www.theworkslondon.com
Josh Robinson

Thomson Lowe
29 Stafford Street,
Edinburgh EH3 7BJ
0131 225 9733
Jim Duffy

Times Right Marketing
Suite 6F, Gatwick House, Peeks Brook
Lane, Horley, Surrey RH6 9ST
01293 772111
www.trm.co.uk
John Gallie

**Vallance Carruthers Coleman
Priest**
Greencoat House, 15 Francis Street,
Victoria, London SW1P 1DH
020 7255 0200
www.vccp.com
Caroline Palmer

Wallis Tomlinson
36-37 Cox Street, St Paul's Square,
Birmingham, West Midlands B3 1RD
0121 233 9494
www.waltom.co.uk
Geoff Tomlinson

Walsh Trott Chick Smith
Smith , Holden House, 57 Rathbone
Place, London W1T 1JU
020 7907 1200
www.wtcs.co.uk
Shanie Connard

Ware Anthony Rust
Newnham Mill, Newnham Road,
Cambridge CB3 9EY
01223 566212
www.war.uk.com
Dale Haste and Richard Bland

WCRS
5 Golden Square, London W1F 9BS
020 7806 5000
www.wcrs.co.uk
Jo Watson

Wieden & Kennedy
Lower Ground Floor, 20-22 Elsley
Court, Great Titchfield Street, London
W1W 8BE
020 7299 7523   www.wk.com
Matt Gooden & Ben Walker

Willox Ambler Rodford Law
30-32 Gray's Inn Road,
London WC1X 8HR
020 7400 0900
www.warl.co.uk
Kerry Bateman

Woodreed Creative Consultancy
49 The Pantiles, Tunbridge Wells,
Kent TN2 5TE
01892 515025
www.woodreed.com
George Campbell

Woolley Pau
36-37 Maiden Lane,
London WC2E 7LJ
020 7836 6060
www.letsgotowork.com
Dean Woolley

WWAV Rapp Collins
1 Riverside, Manbre Road,
London W6 9WA
020 8735 8000
www.wwavrc.co.uk
Andy Wilson or Ian Hayworth

this
year's
briefs

Introduction

The annual ycn Design & Communication Awards exist to inspire, support and showcase emerging design and communication creatives and to connect them with the creative industries.

The awards centre around a collection of live briefs, written each year by partnering organisations and spanning broad creative disciplines. Each brief runs alongside a financial award pool of £2000 and creative placements at either the organisation that wrote it or a leading creative agency with whom they work.

Work submitted in response to each brief is closely examined by these organisations and agencies before a number of commendations are awarded to the most outstanding submissions. Financial awards and creative placements are allocated among the originators of this commended work.

Commended submissions then go forward to a second round of judging, hosted by London College of Fashion to determine which will be awarded a Rocket, the physical award for emerging creative excellence, designed last year by Nick Crosbie at Inflate.

Outstanding work is showcased here in *book*, our annual publication produced in association with John Brown Citrus Publishing, and distributed across education and the creative industries. Work is also showcased online at www.ycnonline.com.

How work is assessed and how placements and financial awards are allocated

Work is initially assessed by the organisations that have written the briefs, alongside members of the creative agencies that they work with. They closely examine all submissions before short-listing a number of pieces of work to be formally commended. Award pools and agency placements are then allocated among the originators of the commended submissions, at the discretion of the organisations that wrote the briefs.

This stage will take place over April and May with commendations being published at www.ycnonline.com, sent to course tutors and sent in writing to entrants at the end of May 2005.

Second Round of Judging, London College of Fashion.

In Summer 2005, an exhibition of commended work will be hosted by London College of Fashion. Over a two-week period, dozens of figures from across the creative industries will visit the exhibition and select the pieces of the work that they feel to be the best of the year.

At the end of the exhibition, the work that has proven to be the most highly regarded across the board will be awarded with a Rocket, the physical award for emerging creative excellence.

Originators of commended work will be invited to visit and take part in stages of the event, further details of which can be found at www.ycnonline.com. Also online are full details of all those from the industry who will be involved.

Rocket

Each year a different designer is commissioned to design the Rocket, the physical award bestowed upon the originators of the work deemed to be the best of the year after the second round of judging is complete.

Last year's design was by Nick Crosbie at Inflate and a study of the design process can be viewed at www.ycnonline.com

At the time publication, ycn have invited a number of designers and studios to submit prospective designs for this year's award. This process can be charted at the ycn website.

Eligibility

Submissions are invited from anyone aged 30 years or under at the time of their submission, and not being paid to work in a creative department at the time of their entry. If you are in full-time education, there are no age restrictions.

Entry details

The deadline for submitting work is 6pm on the 18th March 2005. There is no entry fee to submit work.

All submissions must be sent to:

ycn, 1st Floor, 181 Cannon Street Road, London, United Kingdom, E1 2LX.

• You may respond to as many of the briefs as you wish.
• All submissions should be in the English language.
• You may submit work as an individual or as a team. Teams can

consist of as many people as you wish, but please bear in mind that the creative placements pertinent to each brief will typically be for up to two people.
• Submissions are welcomed from overseas.
• Logos, and other information listed in individual briefs, can be found at www.ycnonline.com.

Conditions of submission, entry forms and item labels

Submission forms, and labels to affix to your submissions can be found at www.ycnonline.com. They must be fully completed. Each item that you submit must be listed upon your submission form. A label must be attached to each item, and numbered clearly if it forms part of a series.

You must read and agree to the conditions of submission available at www.ycnonline.com before submitting any work.

Use of images under copyright

It is crucial that, if you use images from image banks or other sources where they may be under copyright, you make clear in the space provided on the entry form where you have acquired them.

Deliverables

Please adhere to the following guidelines governing the submission of work:
• Artwork should be mounted on boards
• Films, animation and other moving image work should be on VHS tape or in a mac-readable format on a CD, DVD or zip disk
• Interactive work should be in a mac-readable format on a CD, DVD or zip disk
• If you upload any interactive work, you should supply a full URL and details of any plug-ins needed to view the work
• Radio scripts should be typed, and any recordings should be submitted on tape, minidisk or as a mac-readable audio format on a CD or zip disk
• Any additional support materials, written or otherwise, should all also be clearly labelled
• Any models or other potentially fragile submissions should be carefully packaged to avoid damage
• You may submit as many items as you wish

Key dates

• Submission deadline: 6pm, 18th March 2005.
• Initial round of examination and assessment: April and May 2005.
• Commendations published at the end of May 2005.
• Second round of judging hosted over 2 weeks by London College of Fashion in June/July 2005.
• Rocket awards announced in July 2005.

Return of work

Work will be available for collection from June 2005. Dates and arrangements for collection will be available at www.ycnonline.com nearer the time.

We appreciate that some will be unable to collect work in person and may need creative for degree shows. Individual arrangements can be discussed by calling 020 7702 0700 or by emailing workreturns@ycnonline.com.

Work that has not been arranged to be collected by the end of September 2005 will be recycled.

While absolutely every effort is made to ensure the safety of work, ycn cannot accept responsibility for loss of or damage to work submitted.

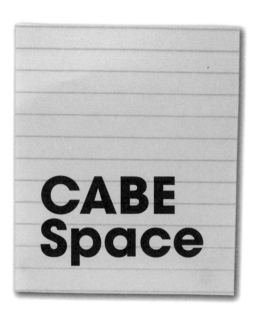

Create visual communication, be it design or advertising, that will raise the profile of public parks and inspire people to use them more

Background.

CABE (Commission for Architecture and the Built Environment) is the national champion for architecture and open spaces in England. Our role is to promote high-quality design by raising standards and expectations in all aspects of the built environment.

We are young, energetic and passionate about good design. CABE Space was established in 2003 as a unit within CABE to focus on public urban space, and in particular parks and green spaces. Our aim is to bring excellence to the design, maintenance and management of public spaces in our towns and cities.

A recent example of a successful campaign was 'What Would You Do With This Space?', which encouraged young people to identify underused spaces in their towns and cities and to dream about what they could become. To find out more about the work of CABE Space, visit our website at www.cabespace.org.uk

Public Parks

Public parks are important for a variety of social, economic and environmental reasons. They are free spaces in which people from all walks of society are welcome. Parks provide a place to relax, play, have fun, socialise, exercise, demonstrate and celebrate. If that wasn't enough, they provide habitat for urban wildlife and contribute to the reduction of pollution.

Objective

We are looking for engaging, imaginative ways to raise the profile of public parks, to remind people why they are important and to encourage them to use parks more.

Target Audience

Parks are important to everybody. You can either generate a solution that aims to speak to a wide cross-section, or target a specific audience who you feel would benefit from such a message.

Creative requirements

You can create and submit anything you want in whichever media you choose. Your solution may take the form of a new identity for parks, improved signage, an advertising campaign, something web-based or anything else you think will meet the objective.

Mandatories

There are no strict mandatories but you may wish to include the CABE Space logo and website address if appropriate. (Logo available at www.ycnonline.com).

Additional Information

www.cabespace.org.uk

Deliverables

You should adhere to the main deliverables guidelines at the start of this section. These guidelines can also be found at www.ycnonline.com

Judging of work and award information

Work will initially be examined and assessed by a team headed by Julia Thrift, director of CABE Space and Matthew Bell, director of communications at CABE.

They will prepare a shortlist of work for commendation and allocate their award pool and agency placements accordingly and at their discretion.

Commended submissions will go forward to the second round of judging to be hosted by London College of Fashion in July 2005. Further information on judging can be found at the start of this section and at www.ycnonline.com

Produce campaign materials designed to sell the benefits of Britain's continued membership of the European Union

Background

Britain in Europe is the national pro-European campaign group in the UK. Launched in 1999 by Tony Blair, Gordon Brown, Charles Kennedy, Michael Heseltine and Kenneth Clarke, it is a truly cross-party organization with supporters and activists in every part of the UK.

In June 2004, European Union leaders agreed a final text for the proposed Constitutional Treaty. All the UK government's so-called 'red line' negotiating positions were agreed.

Opinion polls suggest that if a vote were held today, UK voters – by a margin of 2:1 – would reject the Constitutional Treaty. However, most people are still undecided, again by a margin of 2:1.

The most recent election results showed growing support for the UK Independence Party (which wants to take Britain out of the European Union) and many commentators believe anti-EU feeling is on the rise here in the UK.

Younger people and the very oldest (people who experienced the horrors of a continent divided by war) tend to be more supportive of the EU. Those in their fifties and sixties tend to be most opposed. Men, as a whole, are more favourable than women.

A referendum on the Constitutional Treaty could be held in Autumn 2005 or Spring 2006. It will be the first nationwide referendum since the Seventies, when people voted overwhelmingly to continue our membership of the EEC (EU) – despite initial polls suggesting a significant lead for those who favoured withdrawal.

One of the most important factors in the success of the 'yes' campaign in 1975 was the strength and effectiveness of localised pro-European campaign groups – most major towns had an 'in Europe' group. Involving and mobilising 'real people' will once again be a central element of the campaign.

Objective

To show that we are better off in Europe and that the Constitutional Treaty is about changing the European Union for the better.

To highlight the dangers of withdrawal from the EU and the risks associated with rejecting the Constitutional Treaty by voting no in the referendum – for example, that Britain would be left isolated.

The creative challenge

The challenge is to create campaign materials designed either:
a) To sell the benefits of Britain's continued membership of the European Union (EU) and undermine the key arguments of those who call for withdrawal from the EU
Or
b) To raise awareness of the importance of a yes vote in the forthcoming referendum on the EU Constitutional Treaty, and to get people involved as advocates for Europe.
It should be a campaign that uses creativity to circumvent the entrenched euro-scepticism of so much of the national press.

Materials should be designed with the aim of building and utilising community networks (whether based on geography, workplace, shared interests or through the internet)

Creative requirements

It is entirely up to you to choose the media used, and the look and feel of the creative and ideas.

If you do choose to construct a range of materials, each should be strong enough to stand on its own.

Be aware that political campaigning involves positives and negatives – opinion research suggests people often fear change or fear being left out.

Key considerations

• Penetration. Does it reach people who would otherwise be tuned out of politics?

• Flexibility. Can the campaign tools be used in a variety of contexts?

• Education. Does it give people the information they need to vote yes?

Additional guidance on tone and language is available at www.ycnonline.com.

Target audience

People who will vote or who can be persuaded to vote yes in a referendum on the EU – so the campaign should be targeted, but part of the brief is identifying those groups where the return will be greatest.

Tone of voice

• Inclusive

• Secure in our national identity and comfortable in the knowledge that partnership with Europe is an opportunity.

• Accessible, real and meaningful – contrasting with the fantasy world of the anti-European tabloids.

Mandatories

Election campaign material is governed by certain legal restrictions. Details of required wording is available at www.ycnonline.com.

Additional information

www.britainineurope.org.uk

Deliverables

You should adhere to the main deliverables guidelines at the start of this section. These guidelines can also be found at www.ycnonline.com.

Judging of work and award information

Work will initially be examined by a team comprising of members of the Britain in Europe communications team and members of the different creative agencies that they work with.

They will prepare a shortlist of work for commendation and allocate their award pool and agency placements accordingly and at their discretion.

Commended submissions will go forward to the second round of judging to be hosted by London College of Fashion in July 2005. Further information on judging can be found at the start of this section and at www.ycnonline.com

Develop a more contemporary appeal for Cumbria–the Lake District. Your creative should update the image of the destination and make it more appealing to younger age groups

Background

The Lake District is the second-best known UK destination brand following London. Generally people feel positively towards the brand. Of our visitors, 8 out of 10 have been to Cumbria–the Lake District before, 66% have been more than ten times. This suggests that we have a very loyal customer base that continues to visit the Lake District, time and time again.

However, we cannot afford to rely on repeat business, and effort needs to be made to encourage new visitors to come, since, once they have been, they are likely to continue visiting.

Objective

The ultimate objective is to secure additional bookings for day visits and overnight visits. Raising awareness of the destination is also important, but not at the expense of generating bookings.

We are aiming to encourage people to pick up the phone or to go online to request brochures and make bookings.

Target Market

• Professional DINKS (Double Income No Kids). These are young professionals with no children, 30-45 years old, get-away-from-it-all activity seekers. They are drawn to walking and cycling, culture and cities.
• Caring Parents. 30-55 year olds with pre-school children but who will visit as a family unit.
• Active Professionals. 18-35 year old singles. Urban dwellers who are attracted to high-energy outdoor activities.

What is the essence of the brand?

Cumbria – the Lake District is an inspiring area of natural beauty. With spectacular lakes and mountains at its heart, changing seas and coasts, quiet, verdant valleys, and unique towns and villages, it offers relaxing and rejuvenating experiences.

Attractions include:

Dramatic and romantic mountain and lake scenery
Active outdoors such as walking, climbing, sailing
Low energy activities such as picnicking, shopping, pottering
Compact, safe and accessible from the M6
Picturesque towns and villages
Cultural heritage such as Wordsworth, Beatrix Potter
A varied coastline with areas of importance to wildlife and birds
A wealth of wet-weather attractions
Excellent and variety of accommodation

Research into what people find appealing in our communication has shown that:

Good contemporary imagery and photography is critical.
Chocolate-box images are definitely no longer acceptable.
Dramatic scenic shots are effective. Sunset shots are appealing but do not draw the same number of responses.
Shots of people can be used, however they must be emotive, aspirational and appealing to the target audience.

Media

The choice of media is entirely up to you. You may wish to demonstrate your thinking in one medium or perhaps a range of media. Give thought to the best use of media to connect with the target market.
You may wish to consider developing ideas for print (press and poster), TV, radio, online or other, non-traditional channels.

Mandatories

The destination must be called Cumbria – the Lake District, with the emphasis on the Lake District. To see how such an emphasis is applied visit www.golakes.co.uk

The website and brochure line should be included in all materials.
The website address is www.golakes.co.uk
The booking line number is 08705 133059

Additional Information

www.golakes.co.uk or you can order a brochure on 08705 133059

Deliverables

You should adhere to the main deliverables guidelines at the start of this section. These guidelines can also be found at www.ycnonline.com

Judging of work and award information

Work will initially be examined and assessed by a team led by Penny Watson at the Cumbria Tourist Board.

They will prepare a shortlist of work for commendation and allocate their award pool and agency placements accordingly and at their discretion.

Commended submissions will go forward to the second round of judging to be hosted by London College of Fashion in July 2005. Further information on judging can be found at the start of this section and at www.ycnonline.com

Bring the cool side of Honda to the attention of a wider audience

Background.

"My mum's friend drives a Civic… and raves about it. So much so that my mum is thinking about buying one too. The other day she asked me if Civic did a Honda version." – research quote

This tells you something about that person's mum (sorry that person's mum), but also points to something deeper about the issue for Honda. The quality of the cars is no problem… it's the brand's image and familiarity.

Even Honda owners feel compelled to justify their choice, saying "I drive a Honda because…" instead of the proudly simpler "I drive a Honda." They buy them for the perfectly rational reason that the cars are excellent. Trouble is, 'rational' is in the same neighbourhood as 'sensible', which is only a few doors away from 'dull'. Although Jeremy Clarkson might disagree, it's hard to buy a bad car these days, so emotional pull for them really matters. On that score, Hondas are still a bit low-fat vanilla. Also, Hondas are seen to be for drivers who don't want to use their free bus passes. Nothing against the more mature generation, but a brand with big ambition needs to have bigger appeal.

Objective

To make people feel better about owning a Honda car.

Creative requirements

Some new Honda online stuff. It could be virals, a microsite, web films… basically anything that can exist online.

Target Audience

Normal people who use the web, 30-40 years-old. They've seen Honda ads over the last few years, and as a result are starting to reappraise the brand (a bit). However, it's moved from 'dull' to 'acceptable' in their eyes. They don't yet see Honda as a desirable badge.

What should it do?

It should bring the cool side of Honda to the attention of a wider audience. The creative challenge is to make people desire the Honda brand more, by impressing them with the cool end of the stuff that Honda makes.

It could cover everything and anything including:
Honda Formula One
Type R
Honda bikes
S2000
NSX
HSC (Honda's concept car)
Honda's role in car-modifying culture
Honda speedboats

Considerations

It's important to say that the product stories are cool, but the audience we want to reach with those stories isn't (well, not necessarily). The stuff needs to have mass appeal.

This activity could convey anything and everything from:
• Honda make engines, and look for things to race with them in
• The joy of speed, the rush, just for the hell of it, adrenalin
• Honda is more than a car company
• Something completely different

Above all, it needs to help us establish Honda's belief in
THE POWER OF DREAMS

Tone-of-voice

Honda's core brand values are:
imaginative, human, inquisitive, passionate, plain-speaking and optimistic

Mandatories

Your work should include the Honda logo and "The Power of Dreams" strapline (available at www.ycnonline.com), but how you incorporate this is up to you.

Additional Information

www.honda.co.uk

Deliverables

You should adhere to the main deliverables guidelines at the start of this section. These guidelines can also be found at www.ycnonline.com

Judging of work and award information

Work will initially be assessed by Simon Thompson of Honda and the creative and planning departments of Wieden + Kennedy. They will prepare a shortlist of work for commendation and allocate their award pool and agency placements accordingly and at their discretion.

Commended submissions will go forward to the second round of judging to be hosted by London College of Fashion in July 2005. Further information on judging can be found at the start of this section and at www.ycnonline.com

Persuade 18-24 year olds to re-evaluate their attitudes and behaviours towards excessive (binge) drinking

Background

Social responsibility and the negative effects of excessive drinking are increasingly significant issues in the UK for the Government, World Health Organisation, NHS, Police, Portman Group, media and other organisations.

Excessive drinking over short time frames is typical of the drinking culture in the UK.

It can be defined as:
• Planning to get drunk
• Drinking a large amount of alcohol in a short space of time
• Losing control through drink
• Causing or being involved in aggressive or violent behaviour due to drink
• Acting in a way you regret the next day

 More than 48 per cent of 18-24 year-olds consume the recommended weekly number of alcohol units in heavy drinking sessions spread over 1-3 days.

Of all drink-related issues, excessive drinking has the biggest impact on society. It causes extreme drunkenness, with potentially harmful personal and social implications.

Of all the drink-related issues binge drinking has the biggest impact on society. Partly this is due to visibility as we witness the effect in our pubs and in the streets, but more importantly, with 3.5 million people partaking every weekend, the impact on the police, hospitals, society and themselves is significant.

Furthermore this issue has become a hot topic with the media who have afforded it plenty of coverage.

Creative Considerations

This is a huge issue that is entrenched in British culture. It will require a significant and long-term approach even to slightly move the needle on attitudinal change.

We are looking for fresh and exciting thinking that will aid in continued efforts to move that needle!

You should engage with the target audience at the times that you feel they are likely to be the most receptive to the message.

Your communication should be relevant, engaging and helpful, and should avoid lecturing or finger wagging. You should also avoid an over-reliance on humour.

Target Market

18-24 year olds, especially students, of both sexes.

Media

The choice of media is entirely down to you. You may wish to demonstrate your thinking in one medium or perhaps a range of media.

You do not necessarily have to think along conventional advertising lines (although you are free to do so should you wish to). You may like to consider ideas for events, design, short films, online communication or any other method or approach that you think will capture the imagination and prove effective in engaging the target market with the message.

Mandatories

Must target, and have absolute appeal, to 18 plus (not under legal purchase age).

Must not glamourise or overly humourise excessive drinking.

Must avoid overly sexual connotations or references.

Additional Information

www.diageo.com
www.portmangroup.org.uk
www.nhsdirect.nhs.uk/en.asp?TopicID=14

Deliverables

You should adhere to the main deliverables guidelines at the start of this section. These guidelines can also be found at www.ycnonline.com.

Judging of work and award information

Work will initially be examined and assessed by a team led by Kate Blakeley of Diageo.

They will prepare a shortlist of work for commendation and allocate their award pool and agency placements accordingly and at their discretion.

Commended submissions will go forward to the second round of judging to be hosted by London College of Fashion in July 2005. Further information on judging can be found at the start of this section and at www.ycnonline.com.

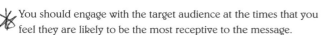

Increase trials of Pampers Kandoo

Background
Pampers Kandoo, the first flushable toilet wipe for children starting to use the toilet, was brought to market in July 2002. Underlying its success is the brand's in-depth understanding of consumer needs and wants. We worked with child development experts, parents and children to understand how we could bring the best product to market.

Pampers is committed to meeting both the functional and emotional needs of parents and children, developing an expanding range of products for these needs. The launch of Pampers Kandoo has been instrumental in growing the childcare sector significantly with the creation of the toilet wipes category, now worth an incremental £14 million.

Consumer need
Pampers Kandoo was created in response to research that shows that children do not clean their bottoms very well with dry toilet paper after toileting, leaving parents to "finish the job".

Findings showed that children found handling the dispensing of toilet paper tricky, the sensation of toilet paper often too dry/rough, and proper usage difficult. A real source of frustration for both kids and mums – children were unable to finish the job themselves and parents were conscious of not disrupting the learning process of using the toilet independently.

According to parents, there is a distinct missing link between the stage where the toddler has achieved potty training and the stage when they start using the toilet by themselves. Parents were eager to encourage their child's development in learning this task but only with reassurances that the child would be clean. Kandoo Wipes were developed for children aged 3 to 7 years who have already been potty trained but are now learning to use the toilet by themselves. The moist, soft toilet wipes, created to be perfectly hand sized, allow children to wipe themselves clean – therefore establishing independence from their parents.

Consumer feedback
Since its launch, Pampers consumer relations department has received rave reviews from mums all over the UK and Ireland reporting outstanding feedback. Consumers not only derive satisfaction from the performance of the product but also identify emotional benefits for carer and child by easing the trials and tribulations of toilet-training.

A winning product
The product design plays an integral role to the success of Kandoo.

Key benefits include:
• Innovative tub design – the melon-scented wipes come in an innovative purple and lime pop-up tub with a toilet seat shaped lid, making dispensing easy and fun for children
• Brightly coloured, to encourage proper usage of the product by the child
• Fun to use – the lid resembles a toilet seat when pushed open, and dispenses one wipe at a time
• Easy to open – the push button is perfectly sized for little fingers
• Secure closure – critical to keep the wipes moist and fresh
• Pictorial guide – the Kandoo Frog character appears on the tub to demonstrate how to use the wipes. Central to all advertising, point of sale and promotions, the character appeals to young children and encourages them to use the product properly

UK Launch Plan
The launch of Pampers Kandoo was supported by a £4.5 million heavyweight TV national advertising campaign. The 'King of the Throne' execution hit screens from September to November 2002. Copy drove an empowerment message with kids and Mums – 'I can

do it too with Kandoo' was the jingle that children up and down the country sing. The product helps them with a step towards independence. This was followed by a second execution, 'Princess of the Loo'. Both versions show how to use Pampers Kandoo and introduced the Kandoo Frog character as the child's helper in gaining his/her independence.

Other support includes:
A targeted direct-mail campaign to all mums of kids aged 33 months. This includes educational information for mum and a fun rewards-based passport for the kids. There is also a coupon for a free sample.

Exciting in-store demonstrations took place across 250 stores. A specially designed Pampers Kandoo interactive stand and dedicated POS created in-store theatre, raising launch awareness and encouraged both mums and kids to experience Kandoo. The brightly coloured stand even included a push button to hear the Kandoo Frog 'ribbit' sound.

PR was used not only to gain coverage in the core parenting media, but due to the breakthrough nature of the product and packaging, and the strong insight around helping children become more independent, coverage was also generated in national media.

Objective
We are trying to raise our trial on Kandoo even further. We know that parents love Kandoo when they use the product but we need to drive as many as possible to try it out.

Creative requirements
We are looking for ideas that will drive interest in, and generate excitement around, the product. It's up to you to choose the media in which you work. You may wish to explore traditional media, such as TV, print and outdoor advertising, go down a direct marketing route or look at a more promotional approach in store or in other appropriate environments.

Who are we talking to?
Kids don't buy Kandoo, it is their mums who are making the purchases. Therefore any communication needs to talk to, be aimed at and clearly understood by parents. Having said that, it is important to build on the positive association that kids have with the Kandoo brand.

Target group
• Mums with kids aged 3-7 (prime prospects are mums with kids aged 3-4)
• Must also be relevant to kids aged 3-7

Key focus areas
'Kids independence' message as priority. Pampers Kandoo is specially designed to help kids' toilet training and to build independence. With Pampers Kandoo, children can clean themselves more easily than with dry toilet paper, so mum no longer needs to check. The Kandoo frog helps small kids feel big in a big world, and is a supportive character that kids can associate with.

Madatories
The Kandoo frog should be used in all communications in some way, as should the main Kandoo logo (artwork available at www.ycnonline.com). Additional Information at www.pampers.co.uk

Deliverables
You should adhere to the main deliverables guidelines at the start of this section. These guidelines can also be found at www.ycnonline.com

Judging of work and award information
Work will initially be examined and assessed by a team led by Pampers brand manager, David Jones. He will head a team of his colleagues and members of the different creative agencies that work with the brand. They will prepare a shortlist of work for commendation and allocate their award pool and agency placements accordingly and at their discretion.

Commended submissions will go forward to the second round of judging to be hosted by London College of Fashion in July 2005. Further information on judging can be found at the start of this section and at www.ycnonline.com

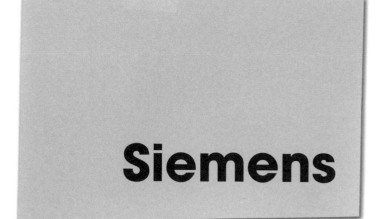

Develop a written communication strategy to make Siemens mobile a more appealing and desirable brand to 16-24 year olds

Background

Siemens mobile is an attractive brand for millions of people across the globe. We draw on a unique tradition of technological excellence and innovation, and on a long-standing heritage of bringing the very best solutions to societies throughout the world.

We are also a very forward-looking brand. Facing the challenges of a complex and highly dynamic market, we constantly review consumer needs and trends, as well as the requirements of our customers.

Siemens produce a range of innovative and desirable handsets targeted at all areas of the market. These range from entry level colour screen handsets to mega-pixel camera phones, premium style-orientated phones and outdoor rugged phones.

Our marketing and communication activity reflects this and is aimed at raising awareness and creating desire across the marketplace. Targeting the 16-24 year old age group is an integral part of this strategy.

What we stand for

• We are for those who seek distinctive style and superior quality in their mobile communication devices.

• We are a strong, attractive consumer brand with an open-minded attitude and a long-standing reputation for quality and reliability in both products and services.

• We offer ingenious mobile phones that combine progressive yet timeless design with outstanding engineering.

Objective

Our aim is to get the Siemens mobile brand further onto the radar of 16-24 year olds and to increase desirability of the brand and demand for the handsets among this age group. This in turn will lead to a higher ownership of Siemens handsets within this demographic.

We currently have numerous activities specifically targeting 16-24 year olds. This brief should look at the Siemens mobile brand and the products the company have on offer, and come up with a tailored communications plan. It should take into account connecting Siemens with this traditionally elusive demographic and create positive associations for the brand. The ultimate aim is not only to increase the number of 16-24 year olds using Siemens' handsets, but also to increase brand loyalty.

Target market

16-24 year old mobile phone users of both sexes.

What your strategy should cover

As part of an integrated communication plan, the strategy should identify the target audience segmentation, the key messages to be delivered, when the communication should take place to best connect with the audience, what media would be best utilised to reach the target group, and what tone of voice is best to connect with them.

When developing the plan you may want to consider how Siemens' current sponsorship properties within football, Formula 1 and mountain biking could be best exploited. Further information on these can be found on our website at www.siemens-mobile.com Alternatively, you may have recommendations for other activity, events, or sponsorship that would fit the target group.

Additional information

www.siemens-mobile.com

Deliverables

You should adhere to the main deliverables guidelines at the start of this section. These guidelines can also be found at www.ycnonline.com

Judging of work and award information

Work will initially be examined by a team led by Simon Robinson at Siemens Mobile.

They will prepare a shortlist of work for commendation and allocate their award pool and agency placements accordingly and at their discretion.

Commended submissions will go forward to the second round of judging to be hosted by London College of Fashion in July 2005. Further information on judging can be found at the start of this section and at www.ycnonline.com

Brylcreem

Consider how you would build a new image for Brylcreem, using the theme of 'Original British Style' and the proposition of 'feel as sharp as you look' at its core. The brief is open to interpretation, but you should consider a range of ideas covering areas such as product development, advertising and packaging.

Background

Brylcreem is one of the few truly iconic British brands. It has been styling men's hair for over 75 years, constantly adapting to ensure its products meet and match the styling needs of men. It is best known for its classic red pot range but this product is no longer relevant to today's young styling market, where it's all about putties, gums, clays and even glues.

In recent time, the brand has re-launched itself with a cutting-edge styling range to become the number one men's hairstyling product.

The essence of the brand is 'Original British Style' built around the proposition of 'feel as sharp as you look'.

These things are underpinned by a number of values that are at the core of male grooming, such as understated confidence, smart looks and sharp humour.

Although Britishness is at the core of the brand, there is no way the brand is going to start flag waving or jumping on the 'Cool Britannia' bandwagon. It is more about acknowledging the positive side of the brand heritage and building on this to give it a unique position in the market which unisex Euro styling brands can't match.

Target audience

The Brylcreem target market is 16-35 year old males. They are guys who care about and take pride in their appearance. However, these guys are not "pretty boys", they're one of the boys and their hair is a serious part of their social armour. They want to feel confident in their look at all times – to be part of the crowd, but still stand out. They are students, college kids, school leavers and office workers, tradesmen, binmen, salesmen... The Brylcreem target market covers a wide variety of professions and we need to bear that in mind.

They mainly read the big lads' magazines depending upon their age. FHM is the major read, but they might also pick up a copy of Loaded, Front or Maxim. The slightly older users prefer to read GQ or Esquire.

Everywhere they go, they're bombarded by advertising from every angle, but they know the score, they ignore most of it and only take in things that communicate on their level and in their language.

Creative requirements

This is a deliberately broad brief and you are free to be as broad or as focussed as you wish in your approach.

You might want to consider ideas for product innovation, new packaging design or any other design or advertising approaches that you think will connect with and engage the target market.

Do's

• Challenge the way the brand is represented on the pack; look at what is working and what isn't. Does it represent the positioning, and if not what would?
• Challenge the rules that seem to be used in the styling market.
• Consider cost when looking at packaging, Brylcreem is a high-street brand and packs that are too fancy just won't make the money.

Don'ts

• Start flag waving about Britishness. Ideas should have a British feel but it should remain as just an undertone
• Be too base. The brand is smarter and better than that, it's more about sharp, clever humour
• Dwell too much in the past. It's more about using this to show what the brand can be today.
• Throw out everything Brylcreem stands for today; look to build rather than demolish!

Mandatories

You should incorporate the Brylcreem logo in your work where appropriate – available at www.ycnonline.com

Additional information

www.brylcreem.co.uk

Deliverables

You should adhere to the main deliverables guidelines at the start of this section. These guidelines can also be found at www.ycnonline.com

Judging of work and award information

Work will initially be examined and assessed by a team led by Andy Rawle and Sam Cooper at Brylcreem, and consisting of a number of representatives of the different creative agencies that they work with.

They will prepare a shortlist of work for commendation and allocate their award pool and agency placements accordingly and at their discretion.

Commended submissions will go forward to the second round of judging to be hosted by London College of Fashion in July 2005. Further information on judging can be found at the start of this section and at www.ycnonline.com

John Brown Citrus Publishing

Create a new magazine for people aged 60 plus

Background.

Since the 1950s, marketing has become increasingly targeted at youth. Even older target groups get referred to using terms such as 'middle youth'. Today, however, for the first time the number people aged 60+ has overtaken the number of teenagers.

Marketeers will have to change their attitude toward older consumers, and view them as a serious demographic not to be patronised or ignored. Currently the few magazines on offer are very 'niche' – for an audience so large, the opportunity is there for a new and innovative approach, whether to a particular segment of the age bracket or perhaps to the generation as a whole.

Issues to consider

- Who is your target audience and how do you appeal to them?
- What are their primary concerns?
- What other media do they use?
- How regularly is it published?
- Specification – will it look like the rest of the magazines on the newsstand?
- How many pages does it have and what size are the pages?
- What type of paper is it printed on?
- Will it be printed in black and white or colour?
- What will the content be and what is the ratio of words to images?
- How will the publication be distributed? Will this be through conventional channels such as the newsstand or do you suggest a more innovative approach?
- Is there an international market for it?
- Is your publication funded traditionally (through advertising and cover sales) or is there a sponsor prepared to pay for it as a customer magazine? If so, who and how would that affect the feel of the magazine?
- If you to go down a route where advertising is sold, who will be advertising?

Creative Requirements

• Maximum of 500 words explaining the concept for your
magazine and the thinking behind it

• Magazine name

• Logo design

• Front cover design(s)

• Example spreads demonstrating overall design inside
the magazine

Deliverables

You should adhere to the main deliverables guidelines at the
start of this section. These guidelines can also be found at
www.ycnonline.com

Judging of work and award information

Work will initially be examined and assessed by Jeremy Leslie
and Chris Parker of John Brown Citrus Publishing.

They will prepare a shortlist of work for commendation and
allocate their award pool and agency placements accordingly
and at their discretion.

Commended submissions will go forward to the second round of
judging to be hosted by London College of Fashion in July 2005.
Further information on judging can be found at the start of this
section and at www.ycnonline.com

Make 5065 the preferred instant coffee brand of students

Background

At Cafédirect we believe that good business makes business sense, and with our range of 100% Fairtrade products, we have emerged as a key player in the UK hot beverage market.

All our tea, coffee and cocoa is bought directly from growers with whom we build long-term business relationships. As part of our Gold Standard Policy, we put a percentage of our profits back into the growers' organisations to support a wide range of activities, from business advice to training in the latest farming techniques.

In a competitive marketplace our partnership means that the growers have the security to invest in their farms and to create a better future for their families.

It's a way of trading that benefits everyone. The growers win, as they receive the best possible price, and the consumer wins, as the best price means we receive the pick of the crop, resulting in tea, coffee and cocoa drinks of the highest quality.

About the 5065 brand

'5065' is our premium instant coffee brand.
'5065' refers to height (in feet) at which the best coffee beans are grown – the line 'the height of coffee taste' supports this on pack. We first started selling instant coffee under the Cafédirect brand in 1995. In 2002 it was rebranded as 5065. It has since grown to become the 6th largest freeze-dried coffee brand in the UK, moving from a niche to a mainstream player.

In order to maintain the growth and success of 5065, the brand needs to attract new users beyond its ethical core. Students represent one such group of new users, particularly as they tend to have a greater affinity with the underlying values of 5065.

Through improving the appeal of 5065 to students, Cafédirect will not only be taking steps to gain loyal consumers, but also engaging with the opinion formers of tomorrow.

5065 positioning statement

'5065' is uplifting for those who grow the coffee, as we pay them fair prices – always higher than the conventional market. It is also uplifting for those who drink the coffee, due to its premium quality and caffeine hit.

Objective

To increase awareness, interest and purchase of the 5065 brand among university students.

Target Audience

University students of both sexes aged 18-24.

Creative requirements

Cafédirect is interested in any way that you believe 5065 can increase its appeal to students. This means we are interested in seeing all sorts of approaches to the brief and these could be ideas for advertising, packaging design, online communication or any other type of method, activity or media that you feel will engage the target market.

Mandatories

5065 logo (available from www.ycnonline.com).
All work should also carry the Fairtrade logo (available from www.ycnonline.com).

Guidelines for Fairtrade logo use are available from www.fairtrade.org.uk

The only exception to these guidelines is that Cafédirect can use the Fairtrade logo on packaging at the following minimum dimensions: horizontal Mark: 27 mm x 16 mm, vertical Mark:13.5 mm x 32 mm.

Additional Information

Further information about 5065, Cafédirect and the way we do business is available at www.cafedirect.co.uk

Deliverables

You should adhere to the main deliverables guidelines at the start of this section. These guidelines can also be found at www.ycnonline.com

Judging of work and award information

Work will initially be examined and assessed by a team led by Cafédirect, including the following representatives of the agencies they work with; Bryan Clark, Creative Director at Lewis Moberly; Brett Salmons, Creative Director at Ignito; Tom Moreton, Managing Director at Fat Beehive, and Robin Smith, Creative Director at Host Universal.

They will prepare a shortlist of work for commendation and allocate their award pool and agency placements accordingly and at their discretion.

Commended submissions will go forward to the second round of judging to be hosted by London College of Fashion in July 2005. Further information on judging can be found at the start of this section and at www.ycnonline.com

Motivate 18-25 year olds to take action and not burn in the sun

Background

Since 2002, Cancer Research UK has received funding from the Government to run the SunSmart campaign. Key aims of the campaign are to increase people's awareness of the dangers of the sun and the actions they can take to protect themselves.

Malignant melanoma is the third most common cancer in 15-39 year olds, and the incidence has doubled in the last 20 years. Each year, there are more than 65,000 reported cases of skin cancer, with 1700 deaths per year.

Sunburn can double your risk of skin cancer, and going red and burning permanently damages your skin, causing skin to prematurely look old and wrinkled.

You should visit www.sunsmart.org.uk for more information.

What is TODAY?

Cancer Research UK is launching a new brand called TODAY.

TODAY aims to engage with an audience that our current brand doesn't reach – 18-25 year olds who associate charities with old ladies and coffee mornings, and associate health awareness messages with school nurses.

TODAY's key aims are to raise funds for Cancer Research UK through music events and other activities that engage this audience, and to raise awareness of ways in which this age group can reduce their risk of cancer. TODAY has its own brand identity and this should be used as a springboard for your creative. Examples of this can be seen at www.ycnonline.com.

TODAY's personality and tone of voice

TODAY has bags of charisma, is warm, engaging and has instant magnetism. But it also has real substance – a strong backbone. It has integrity and a sense of purpose, and is not afraid to rock the boat. It's someone you can trust implicitly. TODAY is straight talking, confident, fun, friendly, intriguing and a bit irreverent.

Objective

We want to communicate health messages through the TODAY brand. This includes the messages of Cancer Research UK's SunSmart campaign. We're looking for creative ideas that will cut through to our target market and engage with them when they are thinking about spending time in the sun. We'd also like to raise awareness of the TODAY brand.

Core Communication

We want to get this age group questioning their current behaviour in the sun, and motivate people to change their behaviour, not just to educate them on sun protection measures.

Primary message

The primary message that we need to communicate is to avoid going red or burning in the sun.

Why?

Burning is painful, looks pretty stupid, will cause premature wrinkles and increase the risk of skin cancer.

How?

Messages that inform people how to avoid going red or burning are that you should:

1. Always cover up – wear a t-shirt, hat and wraparound glasses
2. Find shade between 11am-3pm
3. Use sunscreen properly – factor 15 or higher

Your creative must engage with the 18-25 year olds and motivate them not go red or burn (primary message), give them a reason not to ('why') and can then possibly go on to inform them of the ways they can avoid doing so ('how').

We know that 18-25 years olds…
• Over rely on sunscreen as their sole method of sun protection
• Don't use a high enough SPF factor ie SPF 15+
• Use sunscreen to stay in the sun longer than they would without it, and don't use other protection, eg. shade between 11am-3pm, and covering up
• Are high users of sunbeds
• Have a wider gap between their knowledge and action than in other age groups
• Go on holiday to party and lie in the sun at exactly the wrong time

Creative Requirements
We are looking for creative thinking that will motivate the target market to avoid going red or burning in the sun. Raising the profile of TODAY is also an important part of the communication. How you go about this is deliberately being kept broad in terms of the media that you employ. Please keep in mind that we have a limited budget to put these ideas into action.

Target Market
We want to engage with 18-25 year olds, or anyone who's still in that mindset. They're realists not idealists, keen consumers who love their brands and are media savvy. They live for today but are probably starting to think about tomorrow, and their top priorities are friends and partying. Beauty on the outside is definitely more important than health from within.

Media
Choice of media is entirely down to you. You may wish to demonstrate your thinking in one medium or perhaps a range of media. We are interested in any approach that you think will engage the target market with the message, but again, keep in mind

that budget is a restriction so we are looking for a cost effective mechanism for delivery.

Mandatories
The TODAY logo (available at www.ycnonline.com)
SunSmart logo (available at www.ycnonline.com)
The phrases: "Registered charity number: 1089464",
"TODAY is raising money to fight cancer" and
"TODAY supports Cancer Research UK"

Additional Information
www.sunsmart.org.uk
www.live4today.co.uk

Deliverables
You should adhere to the main deliverables guidelines at the start of this section. These guidelines can also be found at www.ycnonline.com.

Judging of work and award information
Work will be initially assessed by Gavin Coopey, Cancer Research UK Development Director; Jo Power, TODAY Project Manager; Jo Viner Smith, SunSmart Campaign Manager and Sara Hiom, Head of Health Information for Cancer Research UK.

They will prepare a shortlist of work for commendation and allocate their award pool and agency placements accordingly and at their discretion. Commended submissions will go forward to the second round of judging to be hosted by London College of Fashion in July 2005. Further information on judging can be found at the start of this section and at www.ycnonline.com

Increase the appeal of Viz among young adults

Background

Viz is a national institution, a phenomenon that is now 25 years old and rightly regarded as one of the true greats of British publishing.

The popularity of Viz peaked in the early 1990s with sales of more than 1.2 million copies per issue. At that time, only three other magazines sold more – Radio Times, TV Times and Reader's Digest.

Viz was the first magazine for young men and created what we now know as the men's magazine market.

Since the early 1990s, sales of Viz have slowed steadily. During this period the readership of Viz has aged. The present readership consists largely of those who were young men in the early 1990s, and ten years on still appreciate Viz's irreverent humour. These days, the average Viz reader is 31 years old.

The comic, however, continues to maintain a circulation of more than 138,000 and is a fixture in the men's magazines top ten.

Viz comic is published ten times a year and Viz also publishes major book titles. As well as the ever-popular annuals, Viz publishes top-selling titles such as *Roger's Profanisaurus*, the definitive reference volume of English obscenities that has sold more than 200,000 copies.

Objective

To get a younger audience aware of Viz and its associated products.

Target audience

18-25 year old male and female professionals, both students and jobseekers.

Creative requirements

Any creative approach may be adopted and you can use whatever media you feel is appropriate to connect with the target audience and meet the objective.

Feel free to focus on any single aspect of the Viz brand such as the comic, *Roger's Profanisaurus*, or specific cartoon characters. You may also choose to develop ideas in order to promote the Viz brand as a whole.

Tone

Why not get yourself into the mindset of the typical Viz purchaser by going out and purchasing every available Viz product in your local bookshop?

You may wish your work to reflect Viz's unique editorial approach, or you may not. It's up to you.

Mandatories

You should incorporate the Viz logo (available at www.ycnonline.com) and the web address (www.viz.co.uk) into your work as appropriate.

Should you require them, EPS images of a selection of Viz cartoon characters are also available from www.ycnonline.com.

Additional Information

www.viz.co.uk
Here you will be able to see Viz characters and examples of entries in *Roger's Profanisaurus*.

Deliverables

You should adhere to the main deliverables guidelines at the start of this section. These guidelines can also be found at www.ycnonline.com

Judging of work and award information

Work will initially be examined and assessed by Wayne Gamble (Viz designer) and Will Watt (Viz publisher).

They will prepare a shortlist of work for commendation and allocate their award pool and placements accordingly and at their discretion.

Commended submissions will go forward to the second round of judging to be hosted by London College of Fashion in July 2005. Further information on judging can be found at the start of this section and at www.ycnonline.com

Develop ambitious new ways of expressing the campaign "It matters more when there's money on it" that will encourage people to bet on sport through their TV with SkyBet

In 2005, the long-standing legislation restricting the advertising of betting services will be lifted, so that the same rules for promoting all other companies will exist for betting. This means that adverts for betting services can appear on TV and on the radio.

This is a brief to develop work for SkyBet that takes full advantage of this and that encourages people to bet on sport through their TV with SkyBet.

Background

SkyBet is a bookmaker that thinks and behaves differently to others. SkyBet believes that the experience of betting should be exciting and social, and that you should be able to have a small, fun bet on something you've got a hunch on, whenever you want.

Importantly, SkyBet doesn't have serious, intimidating and smoky betting shops. Instead, SkyBet takes your bets through the TV, which you place by pressing the red button on your remote control, over the phone or via the internet.

SkyBet offers live in-play betting on a wide range of sports. These are bets that can be placed while the match or race is taking place. For example, in football you can bet on things like next team to get a corner, or next player to score, by pressing the red button. You can bet as little as 5p per bet. A full list of all the live in-play bets is available at www.ycnonline.com. For a crash course in live in-play betting, watch a Premiership match on Sky Bet Live to hear the live in-play bets being offered.

The work so far

In February 2004, SkyBet briefed its advertising agency Mother to develop an integrated brand campaign which would create awareness and usage of SkyBet among sports fans, and would work to erode the seedy and solitary reputation of betting, and replace it with a more entertaining and social one.

The target audience

Sports fans that have the odd flutter but are not serious gamblers (who they think are a bit lonely and sad). They know the bookie almost always wins, so they don't bet expecting to win, but the buzz of having a bet on, win or lose, is seductive. They tend to be blokes, and all are over 18.

The creative solution

Mother's solution was based on the truth about betting. The campaign is centered around the line "It matters more when there's money on it". It is delivered in an entertaining way that embraces the wide range of emotions you experience when you've got a bet on.

The work features slices of live sport, with people getting frustrated when their bet doesn't come in. To communicate with sports fans, and to make betting more like entertainment than currently perceived, a smart tone, full of humour and sporting fanaticism, is used. In 2004, legislation on betting dictated that betting companies could only have a TV presence through sponsorship idents. Examples of the TV sponsorship activity, press, and event activity can be seen at www.ycnonline.com

The challenge

Given the removal of restrictions on broadcast advertising for betting, the brief is to develop ambitious new ways of expressing the campaign "It matters more when there's money on it".

The best work will encourage people to bet live in play with SkyBet, and will appreciate the 2005 calendar of sport in the UK.

Advertising through all media channels, all partnership ideas, and all event ideas are fair game.

Mandatories

Creative work must include the SkyBet branding, namely the logo and the line "It matters more when there's money on it".

Artwork available at www.ycnonline.com

Additional Information

www.skybet.com

Deliverables

You should adhere to the main deliverables guidelines at the start of this section. These guidelines can also be found at www.ycnonline.com

Judging of work and award information

Work will initially be examined and assessed by a team led by Dave McIntosh of SkyBet and Ed Collin of their advertising agency Mother.

They will prepare a shortlist of work for commendation and allocate their award pool and agency placements accordingly and at their discretion.

Commended submissions will go forward to the second round of judging to be hosted by London College of Fashion in July 2005. Further information on judging can be found at the start of this section and at www.ycnonline.com

However, society's understanding of health has recently broadened from one concerned solely with diet, towards one that recognises that overall wellbeing and the choice of lifestyle we subscribe to is as important as the food we consume.

This works well for Ribena, which champions the playfulness of youth and all the benefits therein. The brand has a long and rich heritage founded on its carefree, positive fun spirit, its associations with happy childhoods and playful summer days.

As such, drinking Ribena provides a temporary respite to the modern condition of stress, seriousness, pressure, monotony and tedium – inactivity and sedentary lifestyles that we all bear witness to and find unhealthy.

Brand proposition

Ribena brings out the playful child in everyone

Why should people believe this?
Because:
• Ribena is a brand that's strongly associated with childhood. Its very presence in a bag or on a table etc. conjures up thoughts of carefree summer days spent in cheeky playful fun with friends.
• Its unique great taste sparks thoughts of worry-free fun that we don't enjoy enough of in today's world.
• The fact that it's still and not fizzy means that it can be easily gulped down before, during and after a bout of irrepressible and energetic playful behaviour.
• Its purple colour is seen as playful, and even magical.

Background to the creative challenge
Approximately 20 years ago, Ribena launched a ready-to-drink format of its squash in Tetra Pak cartons. For 16 years, Ribena's carton business grew, but in the last four years it has declined in sales as consumers have chosen to switch to plastic bottle formats, which are seen as a more contemporary/modern format and are also re-sealable.

Ribena has also met this demand, providing an offering in plastic bottles alongside its cartons.

Make young adults proud to be seen with a Ribena Blackcurrant carton (as opposed to a bottle), using ambient, press or poster advertising

Background
The name "Ribena" is derived from the Latin for blackcurrant, *ribes negrum*.

Blackcurrants contain a wealth of properties not present in other fruits. See www.blackcurrants.co.nz for further details on this.

More than 90% of the blackcurrants grown in the UK go exclusively into Ribena.

In fact, Ribena has a rich heritage in providing blackcurrant goodness in the form of a drink to the people of Britain. Rich in vitamin C (blackcurrants offer four times more vitamin C than Oranges, pound for pound), the product was especially rationed for children by the government during the Second World War, as a way of enhancing the vitamin C in their diet.

The p
are c
make

Altho
appea

Packa
of the
specif

Targe
16 to
an ess
and a
They
the m
Nokia
and p

Core
Altho
reflec

• Valu
• The
• Goo
• Exc
• Inn
• Fui

Supp
• Ph
• Virg
• Virg
• Vir
• Im

All of

There are however inherent benefits to Tetra Pak cartons over PET plastic bottles:

• Tetra Pak cartons are made only from wood grown in sustainable forestry (for every tonne of wood used, a replacement tonne of trees is planted).
• Tetra Pak cartons can be recycled.
• The barrier properties of Tetra Pak cartons are better than PET bottles. Therefore the product inside tastes better for longer.
• Because the barrier properties are better, the product can be made without the use of preservatives or artificial additives.
• The better barrier properties mean that the product does not degrade due to sunlight, so protecting many of the inherent benefits of blackcurrants (see www.blackcurrants.co.nz for details)

For these reasons, Ribena continues to be a supporter of the carton format.

The creative challenge
Make people reassess Ribena Blackcurrant cartons and perceive them as cool and something to be proud to be seen by your mates drinking from.

Targeting
18 – 22-year old young adults.
Since Ribena is a big brand with a broad consumer base, the brand's media target will extend beyond this group, and because of this, communications should have broad appeal and be inclusive in both style and tone.

Media
Press adverts, posters and ambient ideas (feel free to work in one or any combination of these media).

Mandatories
Proposals should stretch the accepted normal boundaries, but should be within keeping of the Ribena core values: playful, full of beans, caring, summer feelings and lifelong friend.

You must include the Ribena logo within your work, available from www.ycnonline.com

---

Additional Information
www.ribena.co.uk
www.blackcurrants.co.nz

Deliverables
You should adhere to the main deliverables guidelines at the start of this section. These guidelines can also be found at www.ycnonline.com

Judging of work and award information
Work will initially be examined and assessed by a team led by Alasdair James and Misel Van Boldrik from Ribena alongside Matt Boffey and Matt Saunby from Grey London.

They will prepare a shortlist of work for commendation and allocate their award pool and agency placements accordingly and at their discretion.

Commended submissions will go forward to the second round of judging to be hosted by London College of Fashion in July 2005. Further information on judging can be found at the start of this section and at www.ycnonline.com

draw
scribble
write
stick